DISCIPLINE WITHOUT PUNISHMENT

Discipline Without Punishment

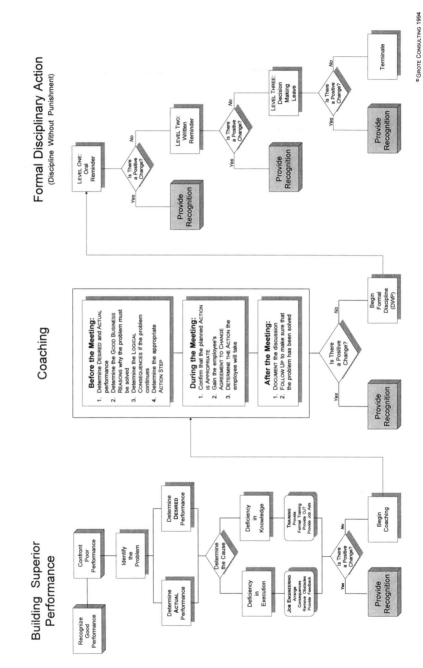

Building Superior Performance

Coaching

Formal Disciplinary Action
(Discipline Without Punishment)

Building Superior Performance

Recognize Good Performance

Confront Poor Performance

Identify the Problem

Determine DESIRED Performance

Determine ACTUAL Performance

Determine the Cause

Deficiency in Knowledge

Deficiency in Execution

TRAINING
Provide Formal Training
Provide O.J.T.
Provide Job Aids

JOB ENGINEERING
Arrange Consequences
Remove Obstacles
Provide Feedback

Is There a Positive Change?

Yes — Provide Recognition

No — Begin Coaching

Coaching

Before the Meeting:
1. Determine DESIRED and ACTUAL performance
2. Determine the GOOD BUSINESS REASONS why the problem must be solved
3. Determine the LOGICAL CONSEQUENCES if the problem continues
4. Determine the appropriate ACTION STEP

During the Meeting:
1. Confirm that the planned ACTION IS APPROPRIATE
2. Gain the employee's AGREEMENT TO CHANGE
3. DETERMINE THE ACTION the employee will take

After the Meeting:
1. DOCUMENT the discussion
2. FOLLOW UP to make sure that the problem has been solved

Is There a Positive Change?

Yes — Provide Recognition

No — Begin Formal Discipline (DWP)

Formal Disciplinary Action

LEVEL ONE: Oral Reminder

Is There a Positive Change?

Yes — Provide Recognition

No — LEVEL TWO: Written Reminder

Is There a Positive Change?

Yes — Provide Recognition

No — LEVEL THREE: Decision Making Leave

Is There a Positive Change?

Yes — Provide Recognition

No — Terminate

© GROTE CONSULTING 1994

DISCIPLINE WITHOUT PUNISHMENT

Dick Grote

amacom

American Management Association

New York • Atlanta • Boston • Chicago • Kansas City • San Francisco • Washington, D.C.
Brussels • Mexico City • Tokyo • Toronto

This book is available at a special
discount when ordered in bulk quantities.
For information, contact Special Sales Department,
AMACOM, a division of American Management Association,
1601 Broadway, New York, NY 10019.

This publication is designed to provide accurate and authoritative information in regard to the subject matter covered. It is sold with the
understanding that the publisher is not engaged in rendering legal,
accounting, or other professional service. If legal advice or other expert
assistance is required, the services of a competent professional person
should be sought.

Library of Congress Cataloging-in-Publication Data

Grote, Richard C.
      Discipline without punishment / Dick Grote.
            p.   cm.
      Includes bibliographical references and index.
      ISBN 0-8144-0276-3
      1. Labor discipline.   I.   Title.
HF5549.5.L3G76   1995
658.3'14—dc20   94-48647
                                                CIP

Printing number

10   9   8

To
Jacqueline

In the following pages I offer nothing more than simple facts, plain arguments and common sense; and have no other preliminaries to settle with the reader, other than that he will divest himself of prejudice and prepossession, and suffer his reason and his feelings to determine for themselves; that he will put on, or rather that he will not put off, the true character of a man, and generously enlarge his views beyond the present day.

Thomas Paine, *Common Sense*

Contents

Acknowledgments

More than to anyone else, I am indebted to a brave group of managers who over the past twenty years have been willing to abandon conventional thinking and be pioneers in adopting a new approach to working with people. At its inauguration at Frito-Lay, people like Ed Walsh, John Pearl, John Ewing, and Wayne Calloway created a climate that encouraged tinkering with conventional wisdom and provided opportunities for new ideas to flourish.

A great many clients over the years have made contributions that have resulted in the further development of the approach. Most recently, John Fassnacht, director of human resources for Columbia Medical Center East in El Paso, a skilled facilitator and culture change master, provided invaluable help and support.

My former colleagues at Performance Systems Corporation helped me expand the idea of Discipline Without Punishment from its initial application at Frito-Lay to a management system appropriate for all organizations. Eric Harvey, Al Lucia, Steve Ventura, and Sharon Middaugh all contributed valuable insights and observations over many years. Randy Pennington in particular added to the development of Discipline Without Punishment.

One colleague reviewed and made helpful suggestions on the legal aspects of Discipline Without Punishment and the various procedures for handling disciplinary action. I am indebted to James W. Wimberly, Jr., of the law firm of Wimberly and Lawson in Atlanta.

A book like this is not only the product of the author's work and study. It is the result of the lessons that were learned about discipline and individual responsibility and decision making in earliest childhood. Without the influence of my mother, Muriel Grote, I could not have become the person capable of writing this. Without the influence of my father, Charles Henry Grote, in whose footsteps I gratefully follow, I would not have chosen this career.

Above all, one person is responsible for providing constant and unwavering support and assistance. I am indebted to my wife, Jacqueline, more than I can say.

Introduction

Twenty years ago, when I was manager of training and development for Frito-Lay, one of the most sophisticated and best-managed companies in the United States, we encountered a public relations nightmare. Day after day, customer complaints multiplied. Each complaint reported the same bizarre problem: obscene messages written on the chips.

All the chips, we discovered, had been produced at the same plant, a plant that in the previous nine months had fired 58 of its 210 employees for various breaches of discipline.

The climate at this plant was toxic. Supervisors eagerly wrote up troublemakers in an attempt to turn the situation around. Employees were angry with the way they were being treated. Some, anxious to retaliate, took their revenge with a felt-tip pen. The atmosphere turned poisonous; hostility reigned.

Like their counterparts at virtually every other U.S. company, Frito-Lay managers had been using the ancient, traditional "progressive-discipline" system: an oral warning followed by a written warning, followed by an unpaid disciplinary layoff of several days, followed—almost always—by the employee's termination.

While this approach was universally considered the appropriate response to lapses in acceptable organizational behavior, we discovered that it generated little but resentment and belligerence. Frustrated, we abandoned it and replaced it with an entirely new approach.

Like traditional approaches, the new approach was progressive: As problems became more serious, our response became more serious. But instead of using punishments, the new system reflected our belief that every one of our employees, even our "troublemakers," was a mature, responsible, and trustworthy adult who would respond like one if treated like one.

The new procedures eliminated warnings and reprimands, focusing entirely on individual responsibility and decision making. The most striking demonstration of management's total rejection of traditional thinking was the decision to abolish the conventional unpaid disciplinary layoff as the final step and replace it with a radical new procedure: a disciplinary suspension with pay.

Upon reaching the final step of the new system, the individual was told that he must spend the following day at home and return the day after with a final decision: either to solve the immediate problem and make a total commitment to acceptable performance in every area of his job, or to quit and find more satisfying work someplace else. The cost of this day was on the company, he was told, to demonstrate that we were sincere in our desire to see him change and stay. "But if you elect to remain with us," his boss cautioned, "another disciplinary problem will result in your termination." We placed his future in his own hands and said that we would accept whichever decision he made: to change and stay or to quit and find greener pastures elsewhere.

The results? A year later terminations at that plant had dropped from fifty-eight to nineteen; the following year they were down to two. The atmosphere was transformed; the obscene messages, along with the customer complaints, disappeared. Frito-Lay began expanding this Discipline Without Punishment system throughout the corporation. Other companies followed suit.

Today several hundred organizations have abandoned warnings, reprimands, probations, demotions, unpaid disciplinary suspensions, and all other punitive responses to discipline problems. The results they have obtained support their decision to change:

- The Texas Department of Mental Health saw turnover drop from 48.5 percent to 31.3 percent to 18.5 percent in the two years following implementation.
- A Vermont General Electric plant, one of many GE facilities that have adopted Discipline Without Punishment, reported written warnings/reminders dropping from thirty-nine to twenty-three to twelve in a similar two-year period.
- GTE Telephone Operations reduced all grievances by 63 per-

cent and disciplinary grievances by 86 percent in the year after it installed the approach.

- Tampa Electric Company, one of the first to follow Frito-Lay's lead, reduced sick leave hours per employee from 66.7 in the year before implementation to 31.2 eight years later. This reduction in sick leave use resulted in a total savings of $2,662,848.

Yesterday's punitive discipline system no longer fits the culture of today's organizations. A recent survey reported in *Fortune* magazine indicated that two of today's most commonly used management tools are mission statements and TQM. It is hard to imagine a corporation pointing to its traditional progressive-discipline system as an example of its mission statement at work. A nonpunitive system, however, is precisely aligned with the values most corporate mission statements express and is a fully appropriate element for a total quality effort. As Michael Hammer and James Champy argue in *Reengineering the Corporation:*

> Creating a corporate value statement alone is useless and just another faddish exercise. Without supporting management systems, most corporate value statements are collections of empty platitudes that only increase organizational cynicism. To be worth the paper it's printed on, a value statement must be reinforced by the company's management systems. The statement articulates values; the management systems give those values life and reality within the company.[1]

As many companies have discovered, Discipline Without Punishment is the best possible example of a management system that fully supports the values expressed in its statement of corporate mission and vision.

Why do companies still use the antiquated progressive-discipline system? Not because they like its adversarial philosophy. Not because it alone satisfies the procedural requirements needed to

1. Michael Hammer and James Champy, *Reengineering the Corporation* (New York: HarperCollins, 1993), p. 75.

support a termination that is challenged in court or by arbitration. Certainly not because of any benefits the system provides. They use traditional progressive-discipline because they haven't discovered a workable alternative, an alternative that is fully accepted by third parties, that allows companies to confront lapses in organizational discipline in a simple and uncomplicated way, and that enhances the dignity and self-esteem of everyone concerned.

The book you are holding provides that alternative. In the twenty years since I first created the Discipline Without Punishment system at Frito-Lay, I have been privileged to work with some of America's best-managed companies to help them implement a non-punitive approach to solving people problems. Some of them have been among the largest and best-known U.S. companies: General Electric, Union Carbide, Southwestern Bell, Martin Marietta, Texas Utilities, Shell Oil, Exxon. Others have been small organizations, for the most part unknown outside their immediate communities: Milltronics, Columbia Medical Center, the City of Carrollton, Utility Fuels, Liberty National Bank. In choosing to implement this approach, they have increased both their internal ability to maintain a competent and highly committed workforce, and their external ability to compete effectively for the most talented individuals available. Installing the Discipline Without Punishment system, they report, is simply another piece of evidence that within their community they are the employer of choice. From each of these organizations, large and small, I have learned new ways in which the original system could be enhanced and improved. Their experience, as well as mine, has resulted in the full development of the Discipline Without Punishment system.

This book will help the practicing manager who wants to become better at the toughest job managers face: confronting a subordinate with his need to change. It will also be enormously useful to the personnel specialist who needs to make his company's existing system more streamlined and defensible. Most of all, however, this book is specifically designed to show all managers, whether line operating executives or human resources professionals, how to replace their current system with a nonpunitive approach. While the techniques and methods I describe here will certainly help increase the effectiveness of those managers who must use the traditional system, my overall position is clear: The traditional progressive-discipline system does not need to be tuned up or tinkered with. It needs to be abolished.

The ideal system for handling the inevitable problems that arise in any organization has specific and identifiable characteristics:

1. It must provide progressive steps and complete documentation so that full defensibility is ensured if any action the organization takes is ever challenged.
2. It must focus on correcting problems and not punishing offenders.
3. It should provide a means to recognize and reinforce the good performance delivered by the great majority of organization members.
4. It must provide a method to confront the few who fail to meet expectations, in ways that maintain and enhance their self-esteem.
5. It should be understood, accepted, and supported by all.
6. Finally, an ideal discipline system must produce this measurable outcome: Whenever an employee gets into a disciplinary scrape, the system must influence him to change his behavior, accept responsibility, and return to a fully acceptable level of performance.

The traditional system is capable of providing only the first of those criteria. Discipline Without Punishment provides all.

This book provides a complete explanation of the philosophy and mechanics of the Discipline Without Punishment system. Early chapters review the birth of the system, the ways to recognize good performance, and the techniques for preventing people problems from reaching the point where disciplinary action is necessary.

Since every disciplinary transaction is a coaching session, I will explore the coaching process in detail: how to prepare in advance, how to conduct the discussion so successfully that not only does the problem get solved but the relationship itself is enhanced. I will detail all three of the formal levels of disciplinary action in the Discipline Without Punishment approach: the Oral Reminder, the Written Reminder, and the Decision Making Leave. And while the need for termination is significantly reduced by implementing Discipline Without Punishment, I will review all of the steps and procedures necessary to ensure that an individual who must be discharged from the organization is done so fairly, humanely, and permanently.

Besides appropriate steps and skilled managers, the success of any discipline system depends on effective administration. One of this book's most valuable chapters is Chapter 9, in which I review every administrative issue regarding Discipline Without Punishment, describe the various considerations, outline the different alternatives available, and provide workable and tested recommendations for each. In this way, every organization adopting the approach can tailor the Discipline Without Punishment system to its unique culture and history.

Moving from a traditional system to a Discipline Without Punishment approach is a major undertaking. It requires the formal approval of the organization's policy makers. New policies and procedural guidelines must be created to fit the specific needs, history, and culture of the organization. The support of everyone in the enterprise who is affected by it must be marshaled. Chapter 10, the final chapter of this book, will summarize the twenty years of experience I have gained in working with companies to help them implement Discipline Without Punishment. I will reveal the detailed implementation process I have developed that has always produced a successful implementation. No company that I have ever worked with to implement Discipline Without Punishment has ever abandoned it.

Discipline Without Punishment is more than simply a better way to handle the sticky problems of shabby attitudes, poor performance, absenteeism:

- It is the fully tested replacement to the outmoded and obsolete progressive-discipline system, a system that was developed over sixty years ago.
- It rejects the traditional discipline assumption that employees are adversaries; instead, it supports the current conviction that employees are associates and partners in the success of the enterprise.
- It eliminates the criminal justice mentality that the traditional approach is grounded in.
- It is a total performance management procedure, one that rec-

ognizes the good performance delivered by the great majority of employees and confronts the few who do not perform acceptably with their need to change.

Your Neighbor's Dog . . .

After all of the mechanics and procedures of Discipline Without Punishment have been explained, the underlying rationale and philosophy of the system can be most easily understood by considering a situation entirely unrelated to the workplace:

> You've got a neighbor; your neighbor's got a dog. Instead of keeping the dog tied up, your neighbor lets the dog run free.
> You've got a problem. Your kids are afraid to play outside when the dog is around. The postman's scared, too—he told you that he won't deliver you mail unless that dog gets tied up. Your garden is being demolished and you're tracking dog souvenirs from the lawn onto the carpet. You know you're going to have to talk to your neighbor.
> When you sit down with your neighbor to talk about the situation you'll have two goals for the conversation. What are the two goals?

When I relate this story in a seminar, the response to the question is instantaneous. Without hesitation, everyone instantly responds with the two goals: Solve the problem and maintain the relationship.

In that simple story is the essence of Discipline Without Punishment. People problems arise in every organization. But the approaches that companies use to solve those problems usually provide only one of the goals.

One approach, traditional progressive-discipline, uses punishment. The employee who has misbehaved is subjected to a series of progressively harsher responses to his lapse from organizational grace. Eventually, he either shapes up or ships out.

But most managers dislike having to inflict punishment to solve problems. They know the adverse reactions that punishment generates and feel uncomfortable with a corporate policy that requires them to write someone up or lay someone off without pay. Not wanting to damage the relationship with the individual, they often let minor transgressions go by. They abstain from noticing that the employee's performance is unsatisfactory and hope that time alone will produce a change for the better.

In each case, the manager is achieving one of the two goals that we hope to accomplish when we sit down with our neighbor and talk about the dog. By punishing the employee, the likelihood is great that the unacceptable behavior will cease. Punished often enough and severely enough, people will stop coming to work late, stop smoking in restricted areas, stop missing deadlines.

But the use of punishment to correct the problem has the concurrent effect of sabotaging the relationship between the individual and the boss. Punishment results in more than just the elimination of undesired behavior, and managers know this. That employee may no longer arrive at work a few minutes late, but he is also less likely to stay a few minutes late when the completion of a project requires it. The employee may no longer miss the deadline, but in gaining that minor improvement the manager may forsake the warmth and good cheer that made the office a pleasant place to be. He may have solved the problem, but he has solved it at the expense of the relationship.

Most people highly value good working relationships and avoid disrupting them, even when the performance or behavior of a subordinate is close to the line that separates the acceptable from the unacceptable. Reluctant to sacrifice a pleasant association merely to promote efficiency or mandate compliance with an industrial rule, the manager is tempted to overlook minor breaches of discipline and run a looser ship. Congenial relationships are continued, but problems don't get solved. Again, only one of the goals has been achieved. The relationship has been maintained, but the problem continues.

Discipline Without Punishment allows organizations and their managers to achieve both goals: solved problems and enhanced relationships. The Discipline Without Punishment system gives managers both the steps and the skills they need to solve the problems that arise daily in the world of work, not by punishing offenders but by dealing with lapses from the organization's expectations in terms of decision making and personal responsibility.

In their foreword to *A Passion for Excellence* ten years ago, Tom Peters and Nancy Austin observed that "managers in every field are rethinking the tried and, as it turns out, not so true management principles that have often served their institutions poorly."[2] Traditional progressive-discipline, with its reliance on punishment and its encouragement of adversarial relationships, is the perfect example of a tried and not so true management principle that has served institutions and their managers poorly. Discipline Without Punishment is, at long last, its replacement.

2. Tom Peters and Nancy Austin, *A Passion for Excellence* (New York: Random House, 1985), p. xi.

1

The Birth of Discipline Without Punishment

For over sixty years, American organizations have been using a common procedure to handle lapses from organizational discipline. This approach, called progressive-discipline, has been concisely described by attorney James R. Redeker in his book *Discipline: Policies and Procedures*:

> The traditional approach, often called progressive or corrective discipline because the purpose is to correct behavior through progressively more severe penalties, has developed into a fairly set formula. This formula consists of a series of steps, one or more of which may be eliminated or added. However, it is rare for the number of steps to be fewer than three or more than five. The following four steps are involved most frequently:
>
> 1. An employee who has committed an infraction is verbally warned and told that if the same infraction occurs again within some specified period the degree of disciplinary action will be increased.
>
> 2. If the employee again commits the same or a similar violation within the specified period, the employee will be given a written warning which will be placed in his personnel file. The employee will be told that, if his or her conduct is repeated within a specified period, the employee will be disciplined again but more severely.
>
> 3. If the employee again transgresses in the same manner and within the specified period, he or she will be

suspended from employment for a specified period of time without pay and will be given a final warning. This warning will clearly specify discharge as the result of another such infraction within a stated time.

4. If the employee again violates the same rule within the specified time, the employee will be discharged.[1]

This traditional progressive-discipline system was developed in the 1930s after unions demanded that companies eliminate summary terminations and develop a progressive system of penalties that would provide an employee with a new benefit: protection against losing his job without first being fully aware that his job was at risk.

Over the years variations on this progressive-discipline theme have developed, particularly among companies in the nonunion sector. Uncomfortable with using a system originally intended for unionized, blue-collar workers, many eliminated the unpaid disciplinary suspension and replaced it with a "probationary period." The employee was told that as a result of his infractions he was being placed on probation for a period of time, most commonly ninety days. He was advised that his performance would be monitored closely during this period and that if he failed to improve, he would be terminated.

Other companies chose simply to issue a "final warning" in place of suspension; others elected to demote the individual to a lower-rated and less demanding job. Some companies even concocted a "virtual suspension," a procedure where the employee is told that he is being placed on suspension and the fact is so recorded in his personnel records, but he is allowed to work during the suspension period and is paid for the time in order not to deprive the individual of pay nor to deprive the company of his services.

Finally, a great many organizations without unions have chosen not to have any formal discipline system at all. Since they operate without the constraints of a union, with its insistence on rigid consistency and the possibility that every adverse action taken with an individual will be grieved and taken to arbitration, they have chosen

1. James R. Redeker, *Discipline: Policies and Procedures* (Washington, D. C.: Bureau of National Affairs, 1983).

not to establish a formal series of steps but instead to deal with problems entirely on an ad hoc basis. When problems arise in these companies, supervisors engage in whatever "coaching and counseling" attempts they feel comfortable with. The personnel department is often called in, either to counsel with the errant employee directly or to provide additional help to the supervisor to bring about a performance change. When the supervisor has finally given up hope of turning the individual around, and the personnel representative feels reasonably comfortable that the file of accumulated counseling session summaries and warning letters is sufficiently thick for the termination to withstand challenge, the employee is terminated.

But the system used in an overwhelming number of organizations, whether codified in policy or simply followed in practice, is the traditional progressive-discipline system as described by Redeker. Assuming that the issue being addressed is not so serious that formal disciplinary action or termination would result from a first offense, it calls for the supervisor to engage in informal "coaching and counseling" discussions with an employee and, when these have failed, to begin the formal discipline process (see Figure 1-1).

The Frito-Lay Situation

The traditional progressive-discipline system was the one in place at Frito-Lay when we began receiving complaints about obscene mes-

Figure 1-1. Traditional progressive-discipline system.

INFORMAL TRANSACTIONS
Coaching and Counseling

FORMAL DISCIPLINARY TRANSACTIONS	
Step 1	Verbal Reprimand
Step 2	Written Warning
Step 3	Suspension Without Pay/ Probation/Final Warning
Step 4	Termination

sages written on the chips produced there. Supervisors in that plant used progressive-discipline for all violations, serious or trivial. Every employee who was disciplined for any reason was considered a troublemaker; his performance was assiduously watched with the goal of finding sufficient evidence of misbehavior to whisk him through the system and out the door. Of course, with this constant scrutiny it was rarely difficult to build a case to justify termination.

Employees working in this poisonous environment reacted predictably. All commitment and camaraderie disappeared; employees worked at the minimum level of exertion. Finally one ingenious individual found a subtle way to sabotage the operation completely. He took a potato chip from the conveyor belt that ran between the production and packaging areas, wrote a vulgar message on it with a felt-tip pen, and returned it to the line. That action, and the resulting outraged complaints, finally caused management to wake up to the disastrous conditions in that plant.

The supervisors were following the provisions of the progressive-discipline system to the letter, but it slowly became obvious that the system itself, intended to cure discipline problems, was in fact the cause of them.

Why was the system failing so badly?

The Failure of Progressive-Discipline

The problems in that plant—the miserable morale, the excessive firings, and finally the sabotage of our products—caused a group of first-line supervisors, senior managers, staff specialists, and me to explore carefully not just the failings of the system there at that plant, but the underlying philosophy of the entire system and all of the assumptions behind it.

The first thing we discovered was that in spite of all the disciplinary action being taken, supervisors were initially reluctant to begin the discipline process. Like their counterparts in almost all organizations, they viewed the formal discipline procedure as the mechanism they were required to use to "build a case" against an employee they had decided to terminate. Since they saw the system as a means to justify termination rather than to achieve rehabilitation, they typically engaged in an almost excessive number of informal coaching and counseling sessions. Even when the employee did not respond to these informal attempts to bring about a change, supervisors continued these unproductive casual discussions since they had not quite made up their minds that the employee was truly hopeless.

When they finally concluded that this individual was not going to make it as a Frito-Lay employee and that termination and replacement was the answer, they then initiated the discipline procedure with the goal of building a case as rapidly as they could. Now resolved that discharge would be the outcome, and seeing the steps of the discipline procedure as merely the hoops that the personnel department required them to jump through to get there, supervisors became almost blind to any improvements an employee might make. In fact, the employee who changed and corrected a problem following receipt of a written warning or unpaid suspension often was resented by the supervisor, who had now lost his justification for firing him. One supervisor even complained directly about a machine operator against whom he had been building a case for termination. The supervisor described all of the "coaching 'n' counseling" he had done and the predictable failures of the verbal and written warnings to provoke a change. But then the employee had returned from a disciplinary suspension chastened and determined to do whatever he had to do to keep his job. "Now I've got no way I can fire him!" the supervisor grumbled.

As a team, we examined what we had been doing and the results it had produced. Our analysis, as dispassionate and objective as we could make it, indicated that there were virtually no benefits we could attribute to the traditional system, other than its rarely needed ability to allow us to prove that the individual had received a measure of "due process" should our decision to fire him later be challenged.

But we could find no substantive benefits that our punishment procedures provided. Our system was failing to meet its most basic responsibility: the development of productive and well-disciplined individuals. Once an individual entered the system, he almost never escaped it. The data were clear: Virtually every employee who received a verbal warning received a written one; almost everyone who reached the point of a disciplinary suspension was terminated shortly thereafter.

It was not just the way we were administering the system; it was the system itself. Exploring the experiences of other organizations, we found that no one seemed really happy with the approach; the enormous problems we were experiencing differed from theirs only in degree. The problem seemed to lie with the fundamental assumptions on which the entire progressive-discipline system was based.

The basic premise of the traditional discipline system is that crime must be followed by punishment. With its constant quest to make the punishment fit the crime and its awkward mix of both retribution and rehabilitation, progressive-discipline is the U.S. criminal justice system brought into the corporation.

But what do we know for sure about our criminal justice system? It doesn't work. The system we were using paralleled almost perfectly the U.S. system for handling criminal deviants, but ours worked no better for us than the criminal justice system seemed to work in transforming lawbreakers into responsible citizens.

Moreover, we realized that our employees were not criminals. They were decent and worthwhile human beings who were always deserving of being treated with dignity and respect. Not all of them had the ability to perform at the high levels that we expected of everyone, whether sweeper or senior manager. Not everyone that we hired had the necessary degree of self-discipline to maintain employment in our demanding industrial environment.

But while some people would fail to meet our standards, either because they were incapable or because they were unwilling, they were not criminals. To use a criminal justice response to their failure to meet our expectations was inappropriate. We agreed that when a person fell short, we had a responsibility to bring the difference between what was expected and what was delivered to that person's attention and provide him with the guidance and the incentive to meet our goals. We also recognized that, in those few cases where an individual consistently failed to perform to our standards, we had a responsibility to that person's co-workers not to allow him to stay in a job where others were then forced to take up his slack.

But punishment—the warnings, reprimands, and suspensions without pay that constituted our system—wasn't giving us what we needed.

Problems With Punishment

The more we discussed the issue, the more problems we discovered with using punishment as a management tool to improve deficient performance:

■ Supervisors often allow some people more leeway than others, even though both commit the same offense. If two employees start arriving for work a few minutes late every day, the manager may immediately confront the issue with the one whose performance in other areas is also deficient. His colleague, with an otherwise unblemished record, is likely to escape with no mention of the lateness problem at all. But word spreads fast, and soon the supervisor is known as one who plays favorites and acts inconsistently.

■ Because supervisors often feel uncomfortable taking even clearly appropriate disciplinary action, they often hesitate until there is no alternative. Then, having put up with the employee's misbehavior for so long, they often overreact and confront the employee far more harshly than the immediate violation might otherwise require. The employee, quite logically, may perceive the supervisor's severe response as a personal attack, particularly since the supervisor has ignored and thereby condoned the earlier instances.

■ Over time, punishment loses its power. People get used to it, and, like the heroin addict who must have an always increasing dose, the supervisor must escalate the punishment to bring the same result. When the workplace is marked by constant censures and reprimands and threats of "I'm gonna write you up," people get used to it. Supervisory chidings and chastenings quickly become part of the background noise.

■ What punishment most often produces is avoidance. People avoid the things they are hit with. If a company's workers see the managers as primarily the dispensers of punishment, they will actively avoid contact with the boss.

Finally we confronted the biggest problem of all with punishment:

■ While the short-term consequence of punishment is an immediate improvement, the long-term results are disastrous. Without question, the quickest and simplest way to reduce the frequency of an undesired behavior is to apply some form of punishing consequence. But the reduction in the frequency of misbehavior is the short-term consequence. The use of punishment produces side effects and long-term consequences—anger, apathy, resentment, frustration—that end up being far more costly than whatever the original misbehavior might have been.

We acknowledged the fact that our first-line supervisors faced an almost impossible conflict: on one hand, we asked them to be leaders, teachers, coaches. On the other, we required them to be the dispenser of punishments. No wonder they dawdled and tarried when discipline problems arose.

At the end of our discussions, we agreed that there was no alternative to having a formal and well-understood discipline procedure. But we realized that it was impossible for any approach grounded in punishment to build the commitment that we needed. The cause of the discipline problems in that facility was the discipline system itself. We abandoned it and created a new approach.

The New System

We retained the progressive aspect of the traditional approach. But we redesigned all of the steps of the system to eliminate punishment and concentrate on personal responsibility and decision making.

The first two steps of the approach we had been using, the verbal and written warning or reprimand, were revised and renamed. Now when coaching and counseling failed and an employee entered the formal discipline system, the first discipline transaction was an *Oral Reminder*. Instead of being reprimanded for what he had done, or warned about what would happen the next time he transgressed, the individual was now reminded of two things:

1. *The company's expectations.* He and his boss again reviewed the performance expectation or job standard that he was failing to meet. If the issue was one of attendance, they went over his attendance record and the company's expectation that every employee

would show up every day. If the issue dealt with a conduct or behavior issue, his supervisor explained exactly why it was important that the rule he had violated must be followed. If his performance was the issue, the supervisor described exactly what was expected in quality and quantity of work.

2. *His personal responsibility.* Besides reminding the employee of exactly what performance was expected, the supervisor also reminded him of something equally important: that it was he who was responsible for meeting the company's standards. He was told in a friendly and supportive, but also serious and businesslike, way that the company had delivered on its share of the bargain by giving him a good job at excellent pay, together with the tools, training, and support required to do it well. Now he had to live up to his responsibility by actually doing what was expected, and doing it well.

The purpose of the supervisor's discussion was not to deliver a reprimand or warning, but to make sure that the employee fully understood what was expected and that it was his responsibility to deliver.

During the conversation he was told that this Oral Reminder was the first step of the company's formal discipline process (something that had earlier been explained to him and all other employees when the system was officially installed). He was told that any further problems would lead to a Written Reminder. On the other hand, he was also advised that if he cleaned up his act and no further incidents requiring disciplinary action arose within the next six months, then this action would be deactivated. His slate could be wiped clean.

The second step of our new procedure we called the *Written Reminder*. It almost exactly paralleled the first step. The supervisor again met with the individual privately, reviewed the situation, and reminded him once again of both the performance expectation and his responsibility for meeting it. Because the situation had now become more serious, he was told that he would be receiving a memo after the meeting documenting the transaction. While this memo would be placed in his personnel file, he could earn the right to have it deactivated and removed if he went one year with no further disciplinary problems.

Making Substantive Changes

Changing the steps from oral and written warnings to reminders involved more than mere semantic sleight of hand. The changes were substantive, both in the procedures followed and in the discussions that were held. Previously, for example, when a supervisor decided that a second-step disciplinary transaction was required, he would fill out a preprinted warning notice form, call the employee into the office, hand it to him, and say something usually no more gracious than, "Here. . . . Now what have you got to say for yourself?" The employee at this point felt indicted, tried, and convicted without ever having been allowed to say a word in his own defense.

After a few moments of sullen silence or acrimonious argument, the supervisor would then tell the employee to shape up and demand that he sign the notice. The employee would refuse; the supervisor would write down that he refused to sign, and then send him back to work.

(And we wondered why this approach was failing to build a cadre of organization members who were genuinely committed to the company and its goals!)

In the Discipline Without Punishment approach, the supervisor would begin the step-2 transaction not by writing but by talking. We told him to bring the employee into the office, explain the problem, and then listen to what the employee had to say. After confirming that the issue was genuinely one of failure to meet the company's expectations and not a mutual misunderstanding, the supervisor then would remind the employee of exactly what the company was looking for and his responsibility to perform as expected. He would then seek to gain the employee's agreement that this would be the last time that the problem would need to be discussed. Upon gaining agreement, the supervisor and the employee would jointly discuss the action that the employee would take to put the problem behind him.

At the end of the conversation the supervisor would advise the individual that, because of the seriousness of the situation and their earlier unsuccessful efforts to resolve it, this transaction was a formal Written Reminder. He would then close the meeting by again reconfirming the employee's commitment that this was the last time they would ever need to talk about the matter.

Following the meeting he would write a memo to the employee, documenting the discussion and the employee's agreement to improve. We believed that using a memo form to document the transaction, rather than a preprinted "turkey ticket" (as employees called it), would cause people to react less negatively to the formal documentation. They might in fact actually read what the supervisor had written. Writing the memo after the meeting allowed the supervisor to record not only the existence and the history of the problem, but also, much more important, the employee's commitment to correct the situation and perform properly in the future.

We looked for any procedures we could find that would increase the odds that the employee would in fact decide to change and correct the problem, without compromising the integrity of the discipline system itself or its ability to support the appropriateness of a termination if challenged. For example, we decided to create a formal mechanism that would allow an individual to deactivate a disciplinary step and get it removed from his file, believing that this would provide a significant incentive for anyone who did get into a disciplinary scrape to clean up his act. We also believed that we could deal on an ad hoc basis with the few game players who tried to tinker with the system by shaping up only enough to get through the guideline period and then repeating their earlier misbehavior.

In order to give the majority of our people an incentive to change and correct the problem, we consciously accepted the risk that a small number might deliberately attempt to manipulate the system. We thus were operating in a way exactly opposite to that of most organizations. The approach most companies take is to create systems that provide the greatest possible protection from the minuscule number of employees who are genuinely bad actors and who should be removed from the organization. But in seeking maximum protection as the goal, they often create approaches that are inappropriate for the great majority of their employees. The many must suffer, the organization decides, so that we may protect ourselves against the irresponsible few.

Our new system, on the other hand, by allowing people the chance to wipe the slate clean, gives the great majority of employees who are responsible the ability to get an unfortunate incident out of their record. Even for the great bulk of organization members who never create any disciplinary problems, allowing them a "wiping the slate clean" procedure clearly confirms that when the organization speaks of its belief that members of the organization are mature adults who are responsible and trustworthy, it is speaking with sincerity and candor and not with forked tongue.

Decision Making Leave

While the changes we made to the early steps were important, the radical change came in the final step of our new procedure: the Decision Making Leave.

In reviewing both our existing procedures and every imaginable alternative, we realized that using a suspension from work as a final disciplinary step had enormous advantages over any other final-step tactic we could come up with. A suspension allows a cooling-off period so that both sides can calmly reflect on the situation. It gives both supervisor and subordinate time to think. By suspending the employee and doing without his services for the period of time he is away, we clearly communicate that we are serious about the matter.

The suspension period is a dramatic gesture. It should force the employee to gain a preview of unemployment, come to his senses, and decide to correct his behavior.

Another benefit of suspension is its salutary effect on other members of the organization. Employees who have been flirting with the discipline system will see the action that has been taken with this individual as a signal to them that the company does not put up with unacceptable behavior or shoddy work. More important, though, is the message that a suspension sends to the great majority of the organization's employees who perform well and never encounter any disciplinary problems. The message to them is that management is not timid or fainthearted in confronting unpleasant facts of organizational life. Employees who do not shoulder their share of the load will not be allowed to slough it off on their more committed and diligent brethren.

Finally, suspension provides an enormous benefit to the organization should an employee ever be terminated and then challenge the action the company has taken. The arbitrator's or judge's or hearing officer's first question is always, "Did the employee fully understand how serious the situation was? Did he realize that his job was in jeopardy?" The use of a suspension has universally been accepted by third parties as sufficient notice to the individual that his job is indeed at risk. If he didn't get the message from a suspension, nothing else that the company could have done would have gotten the point across.

Suspension With Pay?

Suspension, we realized, was the ideal final step for any discipline procedure. But when we asked how the company benefited by withholding someone's pay, we found almost no convincing answers. We knew that anger was the employee's invariable reaction to the three-day unpaid disciplinary layoff we had been using for years. He left mad; he returned mad. One long-term supervisor said, "I've never seen a guy come back from an unpaid suspension feeling better about his job or the company . . . or himself."

Taking away the employee's pay brought another party into the equation: the employee's family. Few people who get three days off without pay are unaffected by the income shortfall. They don't have deep pockets. The loss of three days' pay to a family that is struggling to make it on a week-to-week basis means that we're hitting them in the grocery budget. That didn't sit well with the vision we had of ourselves as decent and enlightened employers. Even if we could justify punishing the man, we couldn't accept the idea that it was proper to penalize his family.

After much discussion, we decided to eliminate from our suspensions the problems caused by withholding the employee's pay. The final step of our new discipline procedure was therefore to be a radical departure from the old system—a disciplinary suspension with pay.

The Decision Making Leave, our novel replacement for the traditional disciplinary layoff, would involve a suspension from work for a single day. While the employee would be paid for this day, he would be required to use it in both his and the company's best interests. He was told he must use the day off to think about whether he really wanted to work for us. On the day following the suspension, we told him, he must return with a final decision: either to solve the immediate problem and make a commitment to totally acceptable performance in all areas of his job, or to decide that working for

Frito-Lay was not for him, quit, and go find more suitable employment elsewhere.

We believed we would gain a great many benefits by paying the employee for the day he would be suspended. Our arguments were these:

■ *It allows us to demonstrate good faith.* We saw ourselves as decent and enlightened employers; we wanted everything that we did in our employee relations practices to reflect and confirm this view. Paying the employee for the day allowed us to send the message that when we said we wanted him to use the time seriously to think through whether this was the right job for him, we were sincere. (Some suspended employees let us know that they felt the company was being surprisingly fair.)

■ *It transforms anger into guilt.* We knew that virtually every employee who had received an unpaid suspension had been irate; most returned embittered by the experience. But our intent, even with the old system, was not primarily to punish an individual for his transgressions. It was to get him to take responsibility for his own behavior and performance. But docking his pay made our words hollow. Paying the employee, on the other hand, usually eliminated the anger that commonly resulted from final-step disciplinary transactions.

■ *It eliminates the need to "save face."* We recalled that most employees who return from an unpaid three-day disciplinary suspension present themselves as martyrs. They return to the job with a chip on their shoulder and a need to save face by talking about how good it was to get away from this place for a while. We hoped that by paying the employee to make productive use of the time away, we could encourage genuine deliberation and eliminate his desire to "settle the score" on returning.

■ *It makes it easier for the supervisor.* We knew that most supervisors hated having to suspend someone without pay. For the most part our supervisors had themselves come up from the ranks. They knew these guys better as peers than as bosses. Their families often knew each other; it was entirely possible that while a supervisor was holding a disciplinary conversation with one of his workers, their wives were playing with their kids together. While supervisors may have understood intellectually why the system had to include a suspension without pay, in their guts they hated having to do it. Instead of talking with the individual about the need for change and the company's expectations, they would instead apologize to the employee for what they were doing, making an already unpleasant situation worse.

■ *It reduces hostility and the risk of workplace violence.* If anger is generated, the risk of violence grows. We knew that we already had a serious problem of workplace sabotage on our hands, created by whoever was writing obscenities on chips as they went from processing to packaging. It was not difficult to imagine the possibility that this same individual, whoever he might be, was capable of other, stronger forms of revenge.

■ *It increases defensibility if the employee is later terminated.* Our decision not to use the layoff period merely as a punishment but instead to require the employee to return with a commitment to fully acceptable performance would, we believed, increase our chances of prevailing if we were ever challenged later on.

■ *It removes money as an issue.* While the employee is away, we want him to be thinking about the requirements of his job, his own occupational goals, and whether the two can be reconciled. Forcing the employee to worry about how he will make up for the pay he has lost dilutes the chances that the more important issues will be seriously considered.

■ *It is consistent with our values.* While it was (and remains) a tough-minded organization with demanding performance expectations, Frito-Lay was also an organization that took pride in being a fair employer and a highly desirable place to work. Using a paid suspension and focusing on individual responsibility directly conveyed senior management's values to the factory floor.

■ *The climate was right.* At that time, long before the development of corporate mission statements and the articulation of organizational values and vision, Frito-Lay was a strong-culture organization. The company was extremely well managed and had a national reputation as an organization open to innovation and risk-taking. While we might pay a price if our radical experiment failed, the culture respected those who were willing to gamble with a novel approach.

What's Different About Discipline Without Punishment?

The Discipline Without Punishment system, diagrammed in Figure 1-2, is significantly different from the traditional progressive-discipline system, shown in Figure 1-1.

Positive Contacts

To begin, Discipline Without Punishment includes "Positive Contacts" as a formal element of the system. One oddity of traditional approaches to discipline is that they make no provision to recognize the great majority of employees who are already well disciplined. The most frequent complaint of employees is that they are rarely told when they are performing well. Except perhaps for the annual performance appraisal ritual, only when problems arise is performance ever discussed.

Including Positive Contacts as a formal element of the system suggests to managers that recognizing good performance is as important as confronting poor performance. It also makes employees aware that the company expects that they will be recognized when they perform well.

Figure 1-2. The Discipline Without Punishment approach.

INFORMAL TRANSACTIONS

Positive Contact
Coaching Session

FORMAL DISCIPLINARY TRANSACTIONS

Level 1 Oral Reminder
Level 2 Written Reminder
Level 3 Decision Making Leave

TERMINATION

Termination

Coaching Without Counseling

Second, coaching stands alone. The common phrase *and counseling* has been eradicated.

One problem we discovered early on in our analysis was the unrealistic expectation we had regarding supervisory coaching and counseling. The supervisor's job, everyone agreed, is to be a coach and not a counselor. The job of a coach is to make performance expectations clear; to provide the training necessary to meet those expectations; to remove any obstacles that prevent the individual from performing at a peak level; to ensure that the person gets the feedback necessary to know exactly how well or poorly he is doing; and to make sure that performing properly—doing the job right—makes a difference, both to the individual himself and to the team as a whole. The job of counseling is entirely different and is best left to those who are skilled at this professionally demanding task.

By eliminating the phrase *and counseling,* we reinforced the idea that the supervisor has a real responsibility to act as a coach for his employees when problems arise. But the elements that would be included in a job description for a coach are exactly those that we expect of a good supervisor of people anyway: one who trains, who gets rid of obstacles and interferences, who gives feedback and makes sure that doing the job right makes a difference. What has been eliminated is the inappropriate expectation that the supervisor should be able to say, "Tell me your troubles . . ." when an employee's personal problems interfere with his job performance.

Counseling is certainly required in the work environment. But it is not and should not be the supervisor's responsibility. The job of the supervisor is to help the subordinate meet the organization's expectations. When the subordinate is incapable of doing so because of some personal difficulty or emotional problem or other situation that is properly addressed by skilled professional counseling, the manager's responsibility is clear: He should refer the person to an appropriate professional for counseling, so that the employee can solve the problem and return to fully acceptable performance.

Most large organizations today have skilled human resources professionals who are capable of providing proficient counseling. Many have created employee assistance programs (EAPs) for exactly that purpose. Small organizations, without a formal human resources department and resources too limited to establish a formal EAP, can meet the need for employee counseling by referrals to a city or county mental health provider or a United Way agency.

While employee assistance programs and other counseling vehicles are extremely useful in helping individuals deal with problems that have an impact on their job performance—alcohol and drug dependency, marital and family problems, money worries—they also liberate the supervisor from having to discuss issues that affect job performance but are not job related. The manager whose company has an EAP can tell the employee who is failing to meet expectations that help is available from qualified professionals. The individual, while free to avail himself of these services, must meet all expectations of the job while the counseling process is proceeding.

Termination: No Longer the Final Step

Another major difference between the conventional and Discipline Without Punishment models illustrated by the diagrams is that the DWP discipline process actually involves only three steps, not four. Contrary to traditional progressive-discipline, termination in Discipline Without Punishment represents not the final step of the discipline system but the discipline system's failure. Termination in DWP is the action the organization takes when disciplinary action fails to produce a change in the individual's behavior that would justify continuing his membership in the organizational family. Portraying termination as the step to be taken when disciplinary action has failed makes it easier for supervisors to understand that the time to initiate disciplinary action is when coaching has failed to produce a desired change, not when they have made up their mind to terminate and view the discipline system as the path to take them there.

Making the Move

When our team proposed scuttling the traditional system and changing to a nonpunitive approach, not everyone stood and cheered. Several managers inside the plant and senior executives at the corporate office had reservations about the possible adverse consequences of this untested approach. Almost exclusively, their concerns about the system turned out to be misconceptions. Among them:

- *Employees won't take it seriously.* There were fears that employees in the plant would fail to recognize the seriousness of the various levels of disciplinary action if there was no punishment involved. But whatever the steps may be, people know what a discipline system is. No misunderstandings arose at all. To make sure that individuals understood the changes and new procedures of our system, we held group meetings with all employees to introduce and explain it.

- *Supervisors won't be able to handle it.* Our supervisors were overwhelmingly relieved with the elimination of the old approach that forced them to be dispensers of punishments. We knew that some supervisors would need more coaching than others in order to incorporate both the mechanics and the underlying philosophy into their day-to-day behavioral repertoire, and we provided it.

There were, of course, some supervisors who resented the change and liked the power the old system gave them to play policeman and write up bad guys. When they continued their old practices, they were advised that the old ways were no longer acceptable. Just as they expected their subordinates to adjust to new policies, so did senior management expect that of them. Treating people with dignity and respect and talking in terms of individual responsibility and decision making are not merely human relations suggestions, they were told; they are a condition of employment. Most understood and changed; a few departed.

- *The system won't be upheld by third parties.* While we were operating in a nonunion environment we knew that employees still had recourse to outside challenge if they felt that they were being dealt with improperly. But we were convinced that our system, even without using punishment, could meet every test of fairness and due process that any jury or arbitrator or other third party could apply.

Our experience in that initial plant—as in the many union and nonunion Frito-Lay facilities that subsequently adopted the system, and in several hundred companies that have installed the system since its original development—is that the Discipline Without Punishment procedure is fully supported as a valid discipline system that provides all due process and fairness requirements.

■ *Good employees will resent it.* This was a serious concern. Would the great majority of our employees, the ones who never created any disciplinary problems, resent it when their less committed colleagues received a day off with pay?

We tracked that concern carefully and discovered that it was never a serious consideration. As long as they felt that their good performance was recognized and appreciated by the company, the great majority of employees couldn't care less how we handled disciplinary cases, since they were never directly affected by the system.

We did, however, discover just what an organization's excellent performers do take great offense at: a supervisor who discovers an employee who malingers or shirks or evades his responsibilities and chooses to do nothing about it. By creating a discipline system that was more palatable for our weaker supervisors, we allowed those who in the past might have avoided a disciplinary confrontation to confront problems appropriately.

■ *People will take advantage of it to get an extra paid day off.* This concern we had no difficulty confronting. On the day we announced the change, several employees facetiously confronted their supervisors with the question, "Hey! Does this mean that if I screw up enough I can get a free day off?" The supervisor laughed and said yes, adding, "I can get you one right now. . . . Do you want it?" Of course, no one did. Even the worst organizational game-players quickly realized that there were easier ways to get a "free day off" than by going to the final step of the discipline system.

■ *We will lose our power to control employee behavior.* Managers who were comfortable with their parental role were hesitant to embrace a system that placed all the responsibility for performance with the employee. But the idea that managers can actually control the behavior of their subordinates is a myth. While they certainly can influence what people choose to do, the absolute control of behavior resides always within each individual. The decision to perform well or to perform poorly, to follow the organization's rules or to flout them, is always the employee's. The Discipline Without Punishment approach not only encourages individual responsibility but in fact demands it.

■ *It rewards misbehavior.* This remains one of the most common and deep-seated reservations about the system. Many managers have an ingrained attitude that punishment is the only appropriate response to employee failings in performance and behavior. They perceive that the failure to respond ruthlessly when someone has acted inappropriately is a demonstration of a gutless and faint-hearted refusal to do what needs to be done.

What they fail to see is that requiring someone to take personal responsibility for his own behavior is a far tougher response than merely handing out a punishment.

If the system indeed rewards misbehavior, then we would expect the hundreds of companies that have implemented the approach since it was first developed at Frito-Lay to be reporting an enormous overabundance of misbehavior. They don't. They report the opposite. Discipline Without Punishment does not reward misbehavior; it confronts it. It confronts misbehavior not merely with punishment, which, at best, generates only compliance. It confronts misbehavior with the demand that the errant employee take personal responsibility for what he has done, make a personal decision to either correct the problem or leave the company, and then live up to the decision he has made.

The Results

Between the first of January and the end of September 1973, fifty-eight employees in that Frito-Lay plant were fired for disciplinary reasons. We developed the system in October and November and installed it just before the first of the year. All supervisors were trained; all employees attended orientation programs. We were frank about the fact that we had problems and needed everyone's help. On January 1, the new approach went on-line.

Nine months went by. By October 1, the fifty-eight terminations of the year before had dropped to nineteen. Morale had improved as supervisors abandoned punitive responses and began dealing with problems in a mature and dignified way. Recognition of good performance increased markedly. The atmosphere was no longer toxic. People felt the plant was now a good place to work. Obscene messages on chips disappeared.

Another year went by. Terminations for the whole year totalled only two. The plant was transformed. Managers in other plants started visiting to see what we had done. They started implementing the approach in their locations and discovered that it worked as well in places where there weren't any problems as it had in our plant. Sales and accounting operations started putting in the system. Other companies had heard about what was going on at Frito-Lay and were calling for information. The word was spreading.

Fostering Employee Dignity and Self-Respect

In the twenty years since the Discipline Without Punishment approach was first developed at Frito-Lay, hundreds of organizations have adopted it. In almost no other case, however, has the impetus for change been the need to overcome the horrendous problems of morale and sabotage that existed where it was created. Organizations that implement the system today do so not because they have problems but because they don't. They find that this approach fits their vision of how an organization that values dignity and respect, individual responsibility and self-esteem deals with the inevitable problems of organizational life.

The traditional progressive-discipline system in the United States, created by reluctant organizations in response to union demands, mirrors the values and attitudes of the time in which it emerged. This process—verbal warning, written warning, suspension without pay, termination—reflects the obsolete notion that labor and management are adversaries.

Today, progressive-discipline is the only vestige of traditional labor-management thinking remaining in most organizations. No other personnel practice has remained in use unchanged for sixty years. No other human resources system reflects the antagonistic assumption that employees and managers are enemies.

The traditional system actually reinforces a belief system that most organizations are actively working to abolish. We no longer refer to "labor"; today we talk of "employees." Many companies, in fact, are abandoning the "employee" label altogether in favor of "associate." Yesterday's "personnel department" is today's "human resources." Tomorrow it may be the "People Department" if the lead of several major organizations is followed.

Making Workers More Responsible

But the traditional system is flawed by more than just its exclusive reliance on punishment and its outmoded assumptions about people and work. Its major shortcoming is that it is insufficiently demanding.

To most people, punishment seems like a tough way of assuring compliance with organizational standards. If someone fails to meet expectations, we punish that individual until he complies.

But compliance is all that the traditional system can produce, and organizations today need more than mere compliance. While we can punish people into compliance, we cannot punish people into commitment. And genuine commitment to the organization and its goals is what Discipline Without Punishment can produce.

The greatest difficulty with the traditional punitive approach is that it asks too little. When an employee receives a warning or reprimand, he is simply scolded for what he has done and threatened with greater retribution should he choose to continue. No formal commitment to change has been asked or provided. The employee who receives a disciplinary layoff without pay is not required to use that time to consider seriously what he wants out of a job; he is merely asked to serve out his sentence.

But the individual who receives an Oral or Written Reminder under the Discipline Without Punishment approach is not punished for the past. He is formally reminded of what the organization expects of him, and, equally as important, reminded that it is his responsibility to meet the company's expectations and do what he is getting paid to do. The individual who is placed on a Decision Making Leave suffers no punishment: He is not docked his pay for the time he is gone; he does not have to dip into meager savings to keep food on the table while he is suspended from work. But he is faced with a far tougher responsibility than making a few days' financial adjustment because of his loss of a paycheck. He is required to return to work with a commitment: to change and remain part of the family, or decide that this is not the right place and move on. He does not merely return to his desk or machine or workstation having simply served out his time. He stands before his boss and announces the decision he has come to about his own future and his future performance.

The traditional progressive-discipline system takes a problem employee, punishes him, and leaves the organization with a punished problem employee. The Discipline Without Punishment system requires the problem employee to become one of two things: either a good employee or an ex-employee.

Part One

Building Superior Performance

Building Superior Performance

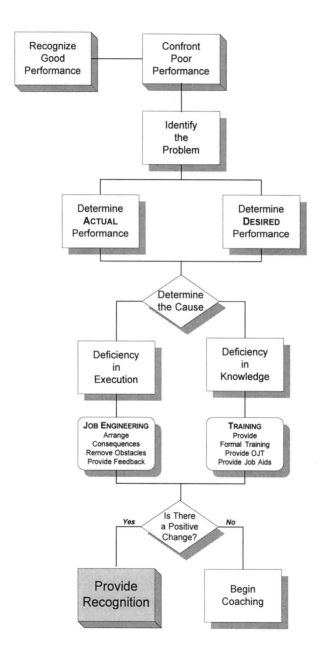

2

Recognizing Good Performance

To create a well-disciplined organization, the manager has two primary responsibilities: to recognize and reinforce good performance, and to confront and correct poor performance.

Conducting disciplinary discussions is a very minor part of any manager's performance management efforts. Time spent on recognizing the good performance generated daily by the great majority of organization members will result in far less time spent on problem solving. And problem-solving efforts at the earliest training and coaching stages will result in far less time spent later in disciplinary discussions.

The Discipline Without Punishment system begins by recognizing that the overall objective of the enterprise's discipline system should properly be the development of well-disciplined individuals who are committed to the organization, its mission, its values, and its vision. As a result, the first element of Discipline Without Punishment is Positive Contacts, the recognition of good performance.

Building superior organizational performance begins with the awareness that the great majority of organization members are committed, dedicated, and well disciplined. While there may occasionally be a need for coaching to enhance a level of performance that is already fully acceptable, or a need for training as new technologies and procedures supplant old, or a need for casual conversations to redirect performance that has gone slightly off track, the manager's primary responsibility in managing performance should be to reinforce the existing level of fully respectable and fitting performance already provided by organization members. In Discipline Without

Punishment this recognition of good performance is a formal element of the system—a Positive Contact. The result of using Positive Contacts is the development of motivation.

Explaining Motivation

What explains human behavior? How can we predict what someone will do? How do we get people to do what we want them to do?

All of us are individuals; no two people are the same. There is, however, one observation about people and their behavior that seems to be true most of the time: *Behavior is a function of its consequences.*

This statement asserts that a person's behavior—the things that a person does and says—is influenced to a large extent by what happens to that person as a result. In simpler terms: *Behavior rewarded is behavior repeated.* People do things based on what happens to them as a result of what they do.

Psychologists call this idea "positive reinforcement." It works in a straightforward way:

- If a person does something and discovers that the result, the consequence, is *positive* (pleasant, rewarding, desirable), he or she is likely to do that thing again.
- If a person does something and discovers that the consequence is *negative* (unpleasant, distasteful, punishing), the person will quickly stop doing that thing.
- And if someone does something and discovers that the consequences are nonexistent—in other words, nothing at all happens—that person will eventually stop doing that thing.

The theory behind positive reinforcement is simple: If a person does something that we like, he's more likely to keep on doing that thing if we make sure that there is some positive consequence when he does it. By reinforcing the behavior, we make it more likely that it will continue to occur.

Similarly, if a behavior is punished it will disappear, although punishment, as discussed in the previous chapter, generates many additional undesired consequences. Finally, the person who does something and discovers that there are no consequences will eventually give up that behavior.

A personal example will make the theory clear. In March of 1972 I began a new job as head of all training and management development efforts for Frito-Lay. On my first day at work my boss, in the course of reviewing my duties and his expectations, explained that he needed a weekly report every Friday summarizing the activities of my department for that week.

A simple request. Week after week I submitted the report: complete, succinct, thorough. While he never commented on the report, I continued to prepare and submit it. It was simply part of my job.

One week, either because I was out of town, or involved in a critical project, or perhaps because of mere forgetfulness, I failed to submit the report until Monday. The consequence? Nothing. John made no mention of the fact that my report was late.

I soon became less concerned about the quality and timeliness of the report. The information got sparser, the submission date later. Finally I stopped doing the weekly report altogether.

Now why did I stop? A shabby attitude? Innate perversity? A form of power struggle in which I attempted to get away with not doing part of my job? While these explanations may be common, the truth is that I stopped because I discovered that whether I did the report well and submitted it promptly, or did it shabbily and late, or failed to produce it at all, it made no difference. John never said anything.

He never said anything until the day that he charged into my office, furious, confronted me with my failure to submit the reports as expected, and told me that I was never to go home on Friday afternoons until the report was in. Until the day I left Frito-Lay I submitted weekly reports on time.

A simple example, but it illustrates the straightforward operation of the key principle: Behavior is a function of its consequences. In that situation, there were no consequences to me for doing the report well, poorly, or at all. For a while I kept submitting the report because it was indeed part of my job, but once conflicting priorities and demands confronted me it was easy to shelve the report.

My boss's response to my dereliction illustrates another facet of the way performance is usually managed. In dealing with my failure to do as he had asked, he created a negative consequence for poor performance: "You don't go home on Friday afternoon until the report is in." What John did was what all managers almost intuitively have learned to do: create adverse consequences for unacceptable performance. What we have yet to learn are the ways to create positive consequences for good performance. As Frederick Herzberg pointed out two decades ago, "The American manager has found an infinite number of ways of making an infinite number of people feel infinitely miserable about doing their jobs wrong." The challenge we face is to make people feel good about doing their jobs right.

Consequences of Reinforcement in the Workplace

In all organizations, the basic principle of "Behavior rewarded is behavior repeated" is constantly at work whether we're aware of it or not.

Meetings provide a prime example. Consider why meetings never start on time. A meeting is called for nine. Those participants who arrive precisely at nine usually feel a little lonely—most people are late. The chairman then announces, "I see that not everyone's here yet. . . . Let's wait a few minutes until everybody arrives." A few minutes later, when the stragglers finally show up, the meeting begins.

Consider what just happened. The consequence of coming to the meeting on time was negative. Early birds had to wait around, bored and lonely, until the others showed up. Therefore, in the future they probably won't be as concerned with showing up exactly on time.

What was the consequence for those who came late? It was positive: The meeting started as soon as they arrived. Their behavior of coming late was positively reinforced, so the latecomers are likely to come to all meetings late from now on.

Here's another example. Let's say that your work group has a major project to get finished and one of your subordinates volunteers to come in over the weekend to get it done. On Monday morning you find the finished product on your desk.

If you don't say anything to your subordinate, you're providing neither a positive consequence nor a negative consequence. In effect, it's a "nonexistent consequence." Your subordinate discovers that the behavior of volunteering to work on a project over the weekend was followed by no consequence at all. How likely is that person to volunteer to work weekends in the future?

Everything that we do in life has some kind of consequence—positive, negative, or nonexistent. Whether we like the idea or not, whether we understand the theory or agree with the concept, it still operates to influence performance.

When people perform well, the effective manager looks for ways to reinforce good performance rather than allowing things to happen by chance or at random. A skillful manager makes sure that employees discover that there are positive consequences for maintaining good attendance records, doing jobs well, following safety procedures, offering suggestions for improvement, and all of the other day-to-day things that too often are ignored or go unnoticed.

Reinforcing Good Performance

In virtually every organization the level of performance provided by organization members will form the familiar bell-shaped curve. While the overall performance level of some companies will be higher than that of others, as the performance of some departments within a company will be better than that of others, within one organization or one department we will almost always find that there is a standard distribution of performance. At one end of the curve there will be a small number of people whose performance is outstanding or distinguished. At the other end will be another small number whose performance is unacceptable. And in the middle will be the great majority of individuals, some of whom will be performing better than others; all of whom will fall between the two extremes of distinguished and unacceptable.

Ask the typical manager which of these three groups he spends a lot of time with and the answer is immediate: the poor performers. These are the squeaky wheels he must grease; these are the problem children who require his attention.

Ask if there is another group which commands his attention. Of course, the collection of exceptional performers.

What happens, then, to the great majority of people who are

somewhere in the middle? They are ignored. In most organizations, day-to-day management attention is reserved for those who perform in ways other than competently, diligently, and at a fully satisfactory level. The manager's attention is commandeered by those that inhabit the ends of the curve; the vast majority who dwell in the middle are disregarded.

But organization members whose performance is somewhere in the middle form the backbone of the enterprise. Ignore them and we eliminate the incentive for them to improve. The message we send to them seems to be: Want managerial attention? Move to one extreme or the other. And since becoming a distinguished performer is extremely difficult and probably beyond the capability of most organization members, the easy way to get managerial attention is to slide downwards on the performance curve.

It is with the solid, competent performer that the greatest opportunity for increasing overall organizational performance lies. The sluggards, misfits, and organizational ne'er-do-wells at the bottom end of the curve must be confronted and either turned around or replaced. The prodigies and virtuosos at the high end must be rewarded and usually are. But the overall performance of any organization or subunit cannot be significantly influenced by action taken with either of these groups, simply because the population in each is too small to make a critical difference. But if each individual in the huge population of middle-ground performers increases his or her contribution by just 10 percent, the impact on the entire organization will be enormous.

When Is Recognition Appropriate?

There are three situations where recognition of good performance is appropriate. First, when an individual has done something "above and beyond the call of duty." Most managers are able to identify when a person has performed in a truly exceptional way and recognize the outstanding performance appropriately.

The second situation worthy of recognition involves those cases in which an employee has significantly improved his performance, either after a coaching or disciplinary transaction, or simply by his own efforts to move to a higher level of contribution. Again, most managers are sensitive to these situations and know that reinforcing the improvement will provide an incentive to continue.

The most difficult situations to recognize are those where the employee hasn't done anything particularly special or outstanding. The individual has simply met all of the organization's expectations over a long period of time.

In this third case, the need for performance recognition is more difficult to identify since the person has neither performed in a truly outstanding manner nor has corrected a significant problem. Instead, the individual has simply maintained an ongoing record of competent, proficient, and sustained performance over time. Since the person is doing exactly what we expect, it is easy to overlook the need for recognition.

An easy way to visualize the three varieties of performance described above is to consider the attendance records of three employees over the period of one year. The first individual was able to maintain a perfect attendance record. During the entire year there was not one scheduled workday when this person was late or absent. Most managers realize that this level of outstanding performance needs to be recognized if it is to continue.

The second individual did not have a perfect record. In fact, this person's record was exactly average. The year before, however, he had compiled the company's worst attendance record and was told that he most correct his absence record or face discharge. He did what it took and is now at the "fully acceptable" level. Again, most managers will agree that providing recognition for this improvement will help sustain the correction.

The third individual had neither a perfect record nor a previous problem. Instead, over the course of the year she had missed only one day of work (when the company average was four incidents of absence per employee) and had reported late to work only twice (again, while not perfect, much better than average). Is this individual likely to receive any form of personal recognition for her far-above-average performance?

In most companies, no. Most managers would agree that her record is certainly one to be proud of, but the likelihood is slim that her boss will call her into his office and say, "Sally, in going over last year's attendance records I noticed that yours was well above average. It wasn't perfect, but that's not the important thing. I know that there must have been times when you had to make a special effort or a personal sacrifice in order to be here, and I want you to know that I genuinely appreciate that."

Since those words were never said, the message that the employee does receive is, "Nobody noticed; nobody cares." People in organizations listen as loud to what we don't say as to what we do, and our unspoken, silent messages communicate as clearly as any verbalized pronouncement. As a result, the next time Sally awakens with a nasty dose of hemorrhoids and heartburn, indisposed and uncomfortable but still capable of reporting for duty if she had to, she will likely roll over and say, "Why should I bother? They don't care!"

Our challenge is to find examples of good performance to recognize. Somewhere between the parameters of barely acceptable and genuinely heroic are hundreds of people who are simply doing their jobs just a little better than they have to. If we actively seek out this level of performance, we will discover an abundance of it.

The Power of Recognition

Several years ago I was asked by the plant manager of a large factory to do some personal coaching of the plant's production manager. This production manager, the second-in-command at the plant, was a talented individual who was driven to succeed. I knew that Alan had started as an hourly employee at one of the company's other facilities and through hard work, native ability, and strength of character had achieved far more than might have been predicted. He had saved his money and paid his way through college, attending classes at night. He was the logical candidate for a plant manager's job the next time one opened up.

But he wasn't going to get the job, his boss told me, even though he desperately wanted to be a plant manager and there was no one in the corporation who was better qualified technically. The reason? Every hourly employee in the plant hated his guts.

Alan was the archetype of the old school, bull-of-the-woods, rock-'em, sock-'em, beat-'em-up manager. He epitomized the "management by exception" philosophy, ignoring all instances of good performance (since, he explained, that's what employees were paid for and as a result there was no reason to comment on it) and terrorizing anyone who fell short of his expectations. He was a screamer, a bully, a browbeating ruffian who extracted excellent performance through a combination of his sophisticated technical skills and his ability to induce enormous anxiety on the part of everyone in his chain of command.

"While I'm not proud to say it," the plant manager explained to me in discussing how he wanted me to help Alan, "the way Alan behaves is OK for a production manager. His job is to get the goods out the back door . . . to make the numbers come out right. But it's not OK for a plant manager to act that way, and Alan doesn't know that. If he gets promoted to a plant manager's job and acts the way he's acting today, he won't last three months before he gets fired. For a production manager the most important thing is production, however he gets it. But to succeed as a plant manager, he's got to develop his people skills. Teach him how to get people to like him."

In other words: Here's a sow's ear; make me a silk purse. Turn Alan into a lovable human being.

I had known Alan casually for several months; we had had several informal conversations. Now it was time to be serious and talk straight. In our first coaching session he acknowledged that he had never been particularly concerned with his human relations skills, assuming that since his ability to deliver the numbers had brought him this far, it would continue to work for him in the future. When I explained, bluntly, that his current approach had brought him as far as it could and was now limiting his career, he understood. He was willing to change. Alan wanted a shot at being a plant manager and running the show by himself. He would do whatever it took to change people's perceptions of him.

We began with a very simple assignment. "Alan," I told him, "here's what I want you to do. Once a day I want you to leave your office, go out on the floor, and walk around until you find one employee who's doing exactly what he's supposed to be doing. Nothing special, nothing above and beyond the call of duty, just doing what he's paid to do. I want you to tell that person that you noticed that he was doing the job right, say thank you, then turn around and walk back into your office.

"That is one complete transaction," I told him. "I want you to do that once a day for a week and pay attention to what happens. Keep a log. I'll be back next week, and we'll see what happened."

Alan was skeptical, but agreed to carry out the assignment. A week later I returned.

Alan had done exactly what I had asked. For the first three days the result was the same. The employees, when they saw him coming, had turned their backs and had ignored him when he spoke to them. On the fourth day, however, he told me that an employee had said something to him that he had never heard before.

"What did he say?" I asked.

Alan smiled. "He said thank you."

We laughed, and then I asked him to do it for another week. "Don't do anything different," I told him. "Do that just five minutes a day. The rest of the day you can be that same old son of a bitch you've been for years."

A week later, when I checked with Alan again, he had more results to discuss. Only one employee had completely ignored him, and one or two had thanked him for the comment. But what Alan was most excited about was something that had happened the third time that week he was practicing our positive reinforcement game. He had walked up to an employee who was threading paper through his machine. Threading the machine was a fairly intricate procedure; if done wrong, a lot of waste would result. This employee seemed to be doing everything right.

"I told him I had noticed that he was really being careful about threading," Alan said. "I was all set to tell him that it really did make a difference when he said, 'Thanks, but I'm really having trouble getting the setup right. I'm losing a lot of impressions. Could you give me a hand?'"

For Alan, that was a transforming moment. It was the first time that an hourly employee had ever asked him, the production manager, his boss's boss's boss, to help him out. The two of them completed the threading operation together.

From then on, Alan started initiating more positive contacts by himself. As he talked to hourly employees, pointing out when they were doing their jobs right and telling them that he appreciated it, the fear that they had felt of him started to disappear. They began engaging him in casual conversation.

As might be predicted, the reinforcement became mutual. As Alan started actively seeking out employees to recognize, they started responding more comfortably and easily with him. Now more comfortable with the group, he began initiating discussions with employees on his own, beyond the limited parameters of the project I had assigned him. Employees, no longer edgy and uptight when Alan was around, made fewer errors. In a surprisingly short period of time the perception of Alan in the plant had changed.

Of course, there were still times when he went back to his bullying, bull-of-the-woods style, but they were less frequent and more appropriate. Now he exploded only when something serious had happened; his tantrums were balanced by his regular businesslike discussions.

Alan's task was simplicity itself: Find an individual doing something right, bring to his attention that he is in fact performing properly, and recognize the employee with a simple thank-you for the proper performance.

For most managers, it is a great challenge to find some specific aspect of a subordinate's performance that he is doing properly and then tell him that he is doing it well.

Identifying Specific Behaviors to Recognize

In my seminars I always ask the managers to generate several examples of an employee who is performing properly. No matter how much I stress the importance of specificity, their initial responses are all broad generalizations: "Someone who's diligent and reliable," they tell me, or "Someone who takes initiative," or "Somebody with a good attitude."

It is as important to be specific when we are recognizing good performance as it is when we are trying to bring about a performance correction, I explain. If we cannot tell employees exactly what it is that causes us to feel good about their performance, the odds are slim that they will be able to continue that good performance. They won't know exactly what they did to bring about our approbation.

"What would you accept as evidence of a good attitude?" I ask them. "Give me an example of taking initiative." The manager who suggests "taking initiative" as an example of good performance has to expend some effort to translate that general description into the far more precise statement: "Someone who finishes the patient record updates that she has been assigned and asks her co-worker if she needs help in completing her stack."

With minor coaching, most managers are able to translate their initial generalizations into specific observations of measurable behavior. The test for determining whether your description of an individual's performance is specific is to consider whether you can make a snapshot or movie or tape recording of it. If you can, it's specific. If you can't, it's not. You can't take a snapshot of a good attitude; you can easily make a tape recording of someone saying, "Here, let me give you a hand with that."

When managers narrow their description of an individual's performance to actions and behaviors that are specific and precise, they often feel that the behavior they are describing seems somewhat small—even insignificant. But superior job performance is not a matter of doing a few things heroically. It is instead a matter of doing a great many small things well. If the manager provides recognition for small stuff, the big deals will take care of themselves.

Guidelines for Effective Recognition

The single most important guideline for using positive contacts as a tool to influence good performance is, do it often.

But in addition to frequency, there are other considerations to make recognition of good performance effective. Performance recognition works most effectively when it is swift. A common mistake managers make when they encounter an example of good performance on a subordinate's part is to delay holding a positive contact discussion until the annual performance appraisal. Not only are the details and nuances of what was done often forgotten, the event itself may be forgotten over the passage of several months. Positive contacts are most influential when they rapidly follow the behavior being reinforced.

Performance recognition is also most effective when it is directed to specific individuals rather than to teams or groups of employees. While the team as a whole may have achieved a goal, individual members of the team may have contributed at varying levels. Make sure that the distinctive contributions of various individuals on the team are acknowledged as well as the success of the team as a whole.

Tailoring is another important criterion for positive contacts. What one person sees as a reward may be viewed by another as a punishment. Some people like to have their contributions made known to the group directly; others prefer that their achievements be acknowledged privately.

Finally, all recognition of performance needs to be proportionate. Both the sincerity and good sense of a manager who praises a minor contribution lavishly is questioned by the recipient of the accolade and others. Balance is vital; fulsome praise for minor achievements is invariably spurned.

Think small is a cardinal rule in using positive consequences to influence performance. Don't wait until a person has performed perfectly to provide recognition; acknowledge the minor achievements that produced the ultimate result.

Several years ago I implemented the Discipline Without Punishment system with the Texas Department of Mental Health and Mental Retardation in all of their state schools. Employees and managers in these facilities had extremely difficult jobs, since every resident was both mentally and physically handicapped, usually profoundly handicapped.

During a break in one of my seminars, one young supervisor, Robert, told me and a few others the story of his success in teaching a twelve-year-old boy, mentally retarded and so physically handicapped that he was confined to a wheelchair, to rise from his wheelchair and walk.

I had toured the facility and met many of the residents, and I knew that getting someone with severe mental and physical limitations to stand up from a wheelchair and walk was a remarkable accomplishment. "How did you do that?" I asked.

"Wasn't easy," Robert said. He then explained how he had gradually shaped the behavior of this boy, whom I'll call Eddie, so that he was ultimately able to take a few steps on his own.

He began by encouraging Eddie to move his right foot off the footrest on his wheelchair. "Don't do anything else," he told the boy. "Just move your right foot off the footrest." After Eddie had managed that task, he told him, "Now your left foot. Move it. Just a little."

Gradually Robert would add one more task to the collection of almost insignificant behaviors that this twelve-year-old was able to perform. Then he would add another. Each time Eddie did something he had not done before, Robert celebrated his new achievement.

Finally Eddie was able to take both his right foot and his left foot and place them solidly on the floor. Now Robert showed him how to push up with his arms so that he could leave the seat of the wheelchair and stand. It took weeks of practice.

Little by little Eddie gathered his strength and learned to balance so that he could push himself up from the wheelchair and stand erect. Robert then described how he coached Eddie to take his first literal baby steps. He asked Eddie to move his right foot forward an inch or two, shift his weight, and then move his left foot. When his left foot came down, he had walked.

"And you did this by breaking the overall job of walking down into its smallest components and then praising and applauding and celebrating each step along the way?" I asked.

"Exactly," Robert replied.

"Why didn't you just save all the praise until he got out of the wheelchair and walked by himself?" I asked offhandedly.

Robert was flabbergasted—and annoyed. "That would have been stupid," he said. "He would never have gotten up from the wheelchair if I had waited. I had to work with him step-by-step."

I then explained that I had asked the apparently asinine question because I wanted to make a point. "I totally agree. You can't wait until someone does a job perfectly before you celebrate and pull out the positive consequences," I said, more for those other listeners' sake than for Robert's. "They'll never get there. . . . There are too many steps along the way. Help the person move one step in the direction you want him to go, acknowledge that tiny achievement, and then move on to the next. That's how you motivate high performance."

Recognition Tools

Robert was able to help a boy with profound physical and mental impairments get up from his wheelchair and walk. For Eddie, the experience of walking may well prove to be the greatest achievement of his life. And Robert did it by using the simplest and most powerful recognition tool available: his words.

Our words are the most important tool we have to influence the performance of others: "Good job," "Well done," "That's great." Simply telling a subordinate that we have noticed and appreciate his good performance in one area of his job increases the probability that the good performance will continue.

But managers have many other tools at their disposal to use in arranging for positive consequences for good performance. Besides a simple and sincere thank-you, here are a dozen actions or items that managers have reported using with a high degree of success:

1. Assign the individual to work on a more desirable job.
2. Give her an advance copy of a new company brochure or advertisement.
3. Buy him a cup of coffee.
4. Introduce her to a visitor and explain to the visitor how her work contributes to the success of the department.
5. An obvious one: Write him a memo and send a copy to his personnel file.
6. Write a quick "Thanks!" on a Post-it note and stick it on her phone when she's away from her desk.
7. Write your boss a memo about what the employee accomplished and send a copy to the employee.
8. Ask the employee's advice about a business-related matter, such as how to reduce waste, how to improve customer service, how to reorganize the work flow when a fellow employee is away on maternity leave.
9. Arrange for him to be given a supply of his own business cards.
10. Let her take an extended lunch.
11. Clip an article of interest from the newspaper and pass it along.
12. Make a ridiculous plaque and conduct a silly presentation ceremony.

All of these can be powerful reinforcers of good performance and, used wisely, will significantly increase the frequency of an individual's engaging in the actions or behaviors that have been reinforced. But of all these, the most important are the sincere and genuine words that come out of our mouths: "Well done," "Thanks," "I genuinely appreciate that."

General Electric's aircraft-engine plant in Rutland, Vermont, implemented their nonpunitive procedure in May 1986. A year later I returned to the plant to do a refresher training program with a group of supervisors. In our discussion about recognizing good performance, one of them related his experience.

About two months before, he began, one of his machine operators had quickly fixed a nasty machine malfunction that threatened to shut down production. That night, he continued, he and his wife were in a grocery store. He was telling her about what the guy had done and, as they passed the magazine rack, he picked up a skiing magazine to give him since he knew the operator was a ski nut.

The next day the supervisor called the operator into his cubicle and informed him that at the grocery store the night before he had told his wife about what the operator had done; then he handed him the ski magazine as a way of saying thanks.

The operator just stood there, choked up and wordless. "Hey, it's just a ski magazine," the supervisor said, uncomfortable with the operator's emotion. The guy shook his head and struggled to say, "You told . . . your wife?"

"Yeah, I told her what you did and got you a ski magazine just to say thanks."

"You told your wife about me?"

"Yeah. I really appreciate what you did."

"You told . . . your wife?"

The machine operator left the cubicle, clutching the ski magazine and holding back the tears. He had just discovered something that he found amazing and touching. Even after five o'clock, his boss still knew he existed. He wasn't just another machine in the plant; he wasn't just a human resource. The tangible reward for good performance, the ski magazine, wasn't nearly as important as the words his supervisor used to acknowledge what he had done.

Using Positive Contacts to Build Good Performance

Recognizing good performance—arranging positive consequences to increase the frequency of desired behavior—is not a way of being nice to one's workers and increasing one's popularity. It is a practical, tough-minded, and demanding management tool to influence people's behavior on the job.

Ask any group of supervisors if discrimination is illegal and they will all instantaneously agree that it is. They are wrong, of course.

Discrimination on the basis of some things—race, religion, handicap, age, sex—is illegal and should be. But discrimination on the basis of performance is not only legal; it is mandatory if an organization is going to be able to prevail in a tough competitive environment. Even organizations that appear to be removed from the pressures of competition—a city government or an electric utility—may not have to compete for customers, but still must compete to attract the highest-quality employees and keep them from being lured away by other employers.

Using positive consequences and providing recognition of good performance requires that the manager discriminate against some employees in favor of others—not on the basis of race or sex, but on the basis of performance—and make sure that only those who have earned recognition receive it.

In my seminars I always ask participants, once we have reviewed the importance of recognizing good performance and identified all of the tools available to managers to reinforce desired behavior, why managers don't do more of it. "There's probably not a person in this room who has been told by his boss too often that he's doing a good job," I tell them. "We are all living in a state of stroke-deprivation."

"Why don't we do it?" I ask.

Their answers are almost always predictable: "We're too busy." "We don't notice ordinary good performance since it's what we expect." "Nobody does it to me." "I feel awkward telling someone he's done a good job."

And while all of these responses, excuses, and explanations are understandable and believable, they miss the subtle but most authentic reason why we don't use recognition to motivate improved performance. Recognizing good performance forces us to discriminate among our people—to separate those who are performing well from those who are not.

To use positive reinforcement effectively, we must not only provide it actively to those whose performance justifies our providing it, but we must also consciously withhold it from those whose performance does not justify their receipt of extended lunches and Post-it notes and more desirable job assignments and managerial applause. Managers have no difficulty agreeing that positive consequences should be provided to those whose performance qualifies them for it. They have enormous difficulty accepting the corollary of that statement: that the intangible rewards of organizational life should consciously be withheld from those who have yet to earn them.

The Treat-Everybody-Alike Manager

I tell seminar participants, "Consider a manager who makes this statement, and tell me if this approach appeals to you":

> I am a manager who never plays favorites. As a boss, I would never do for one of my people what I would not do for all. We're a team here, and I make sure that all members of the team are treated alike.

That statement has an enormous seductive appeal to most people. They like the sound of it. But examine the effect of that approach to managing people and you discover that the manager who makes that statement is actually saying that he treats the people who contribute the least to his organization the same way that he treats those who contribute the most. He plays no favorites. No special rewards are provided to those who carry more than their load.

There are some people in any organization who adore a manager with that philosophy and actively seek to work for that individual. Who are those people? Those at the lower end of the performance curve.

There are others who loathe that approach to management. These are the people who perform at the highest end of the curve. They quickly discover that their exemplary performance provides no benefit. Do well, do poorly—you're treated the same.

These star performers move. Some move down the performance curve to a spot just above the middle, comfortably at the above-average level. There they can turn on their occupational cruise control and coast comfortably. The rest, with too much personal pride and self-respect to coast and frustrated because their exceptional performance is ignored by the manager, find it easy to leave the organization for one where exemplary performance is rewarded.

The manager who takes pride in treating everybody alike will probably never be caught or confronted. He will simply drift along, content with the mediocre performance his department or unit or function is producing. He will never be accused of discriminating or playing favorites. From time to time he may observe that many of his better people seem to be leaving. Occasionally he will notice that people who yesterday seemed to be highly committed and motivated now seem to have lost some of their spark and drive. But he will never have to explain to one subordinate why another subordinate is being treated better.

The manager who works to encourage outstanding performance from his people has chosen a stonier path. On those who excel, he showers all the organizational rewards at his disposal, and he finds many. But to those in his work group who fail to perform at those high levels, he deliberately and willingly withholds those rewards. All mandatory benefits are provided, of course. Those whose performance is at the bottom of the curve receive every organizational emolument to which they are entitled and continue to receive them up until the day they are fired. But the extended lunch hours, the more desirable assignments, the appointment to special committees and task forces, the little congratulatory Post-it notes that others receive are denied them.

And what do these people do when they realize that the rewards the manager has to dispense are not distributed equally? They complain, of course. They gripe about favoritism; they whine about discrimination.

But the manager who has chosen this more arduous path, the manager who believes that good performance is worthy of reward and, concurrently, believes that mediocrity should be slighted and rewards withheld, has the courage to confront the whiners and gripers with the acknowledgement that they are correct.

"You are right," he responds to the complaint that Sally got an advance copy of the new brochure and Charlie was asked to show the chairman around and Suzie got first choice of furniture and you didn't do anything like that for me. "I didn't, and I chose not to do so consciously and deliberately.

"The reason I didn't," that intrepid and forthright manager continues, "is because you haven't given me the right. I wish I could do for you what I have done for them, but you haven't given me any justification. But let me tell you this: The instant your performance is at the same level as Sally's and Suzie's and Charlie's, you can count on it that I'll be there with the same rewards for you that I've given to them. It's your decision."

Our ability to discriminate determines whether we will be successful in our efforts to manage performance. If we have the courage to reward abundantly the good performance that the majority of our people provide, and withhold those rewards from those few whose efforts do not justify providing them, we will have a wholly motivated enterprise.

3

Solving People Problems

For an organization to enjoy universal high performance, it must recognize the good performance delivered by the great majority of organization members. The more that the manager provides positive consequences (Positive Contacts) for good performance, the more likely it is that good performance will be delivered.

In spite of any action that the manager takes, however, people problems will still arise. When they do, managers need to confront the problems and make sure that the individual's performance returns to a fully acceptable level.

Some performance problems can easily be defined in a specific and measurable way. In the area of attendance, for example, the employee's variation from organizational expectations is clear and visible. The company expects the employee to be at work every day on time; in the last three weeks Henry has arrived at work more than twenty minutes late on three separate occasions. In this case the variance between expected and actual is clear.

In other cases the gap between desired and actual performance is more difficult to define. When the concern is related to the quality of an individual's work, or to her relations with customers and co-workers, or to his general demeanor and attitude, it is more difficult to develop a straightforward description of the variance between what is expected and what is delivered. But whatever the issue may be, problems cannot be solved until they can be identified specifically.

Types of Problems

To begin, it is useful to recognize that all problems of human performance in an organization can be divided into one of three categories:

1. *Attendance.* Attendance problems arise when an individual fails to meet the company's expectation that he will be at work on time every day. When Columbia Medical Center, El Paso's premiere health care organization, recently implemented Discipline Without Punishment, they articulated their attendance expectations in a way that could not be misunderstood. Their policy states: "Our attendance expectations are simple and clear. We expect every employee to be at work, on time, for the full duration of the scheduled work shift, every day that the employee is scheduled to work."

2. *Performance.* Conventional wisdom holds that there are four, and only four, ways in which individual performance can be measured in an organization: quality, quantity, cost, and time. Problems in the performance category include such things as failure to meet deadlines, failure to attain goals, excessive scrap and waste, provoking customer complaints, and wasting time.

3. *Conduct.* The conduct arena involves those issues which deal with violating the organization's rules or standards. Examples include smoking in a restricted area, inappropriate use of company vehicles, safety violations, failure to comply with expense reimbursement procedures, unauthorized acceptance of gifts, and theft of company property.

Sorting a problem into its appropriate category is helpful for two reasons. First, these three categories describe the universe of possible problems the manager may encounter. Any problem that arises in an organization will be either an issue of attendance, of performance, or of conduct. It is helpful, therefore, to start the problem-solving process by identifying the specific category into which the concern falls.

Second, it is helpful to note that the three categories of performance problems are mutually exclusive. In other words, not only do all people problems that the manager will ever encounter fall very neatly into one of the three categories, but there is no relationship or overlap between the three. The employee who has a problem arriving for work on time every day (a problem in the attendance category) may do an excellent job while he's there and never violate any of the organization's rules. Another individual may smoke in a restricted area (a conduct violation) but perform at a highly competent level and maintain an excellent attendance record. Finally, the organization may encounter the person whose quality of work is unacceptable (a performance issue) but who maintains an acceptable attendance record and follows all the company's rules and standards.

This problem-segregation process will be particularly useful later on when we explore the administration of the discipline system. One of the most vexing issues confronting managers is determining when a disciplinary step should be repeated and when it is appropriate to move to the next, more formal level. How many Oral Reminders may an employee receive? When should that individual be moved to the Written Reminder stage? If the organization follows the procedure of identifying problems as attendance, performance, or conduct issues, it becomes much simpler to provide workable guidelines on the number of disciplinary transactions an individual may receive.

What About Attitude?

Wait a minute, managers frequently respond once they've encountered the idea that all problems fall in an orderly way into the three uncluttered categories of attendance, performance and conduct. What about somebody with an attitude problem? Which category is that? Or is that a category all its own?

The quest for a solution to "attitude problems" may be the most fruitless endeavor managers undertake.

In Chapter 2, I emphasized the importance of being specific when describing the action or behavior of the individual whose good work you are recognizing. The test for specificity involved determining whether a snapshot, movie, or tape recording could be made of what the person had done. If it can, it's specific.

It is even more important when we are trying to solve problems that we be specific about what the issue of concern to us is.

What is an attitude? An attitude represents a judgment that managers make, a generalization based on the specific things they see and hear people do. The manager sees the subordinate shrug his shoulders and turn away when a customer asks for help and says he's got an attitude problem. The supervisor hears a service representative talking to a customer in a way that will undoubtedly generate anger and resentment toward the organization and says, I must do something about her attitude.

So what can be done? Harold Hook, former CEO of several large insurance companies and insightful commentator on the managerial life once observed, "There are only three ways to make a basic, fundamental, sustained change in someone's attitude—deep psychotherapy, deep religious conversion, and brain surgery. Ain't none of us qualified. Live with what the person is, change what the person does."

The difficulty in trying to correct attitudinal deficiencies is that it is virtually impossible to get an employee to agree that he or she is the possessor of a bad attitude. If the manager confronts the person with the statement, "Joe, you've got a bad attitude, and I need you to have a good attitude," it's unlikely that this will produce a significant change in Joe.

But is it really Joe's attitude that we want to change, or is the way Joe interacts with customers and co-workers? A more direct and successful tactic is to accept that Joe has a right to his attitude, just as he has a right to his name and his religion and all the other things that make Joe Joe.

What he doesn't have a right to do is behave in such a way that causes customers to take their business elsewhere or makes co-workers avoid interactions with him.

What does Joe do that leads you to the conclusion that he has a bad attitude? What is it about Joe's attitude that impacts adversely on the work to be done? What would an independent observer accept as evidence that Joe truly does have a bad attitude? What are the actual words that Joe says? What are the things you would have Joe do (or stop doing) that would convince you that he had solved the "attitude problem"? These are the questions that will allow us to get beyond the concern with attitude itself and focus on specific behavior.

As we will explore in much greater detail later in the chapters on conducting coaching and disciplinary discussions, the purpose of the discussion with the individual will be to gain the employee's agreement to solve a problem. If we define the problem to be solved as "the possession and display of a tattered attitude," the chances are nil that we will gain agreement and provoke a real change.

If we realize that our initial diagnosis of "attitude problem" is no more than a label we apply to a generalization we have made based on the observation of specific behavior, we can then deal directly with the behavior itself. In this case, the odds are great that change can be generated.

To verbalize our unhappiness with someone's attitude directly is usually perceived by the individual as a personal attack. But to discuss the specific things we see and hear is to deal with things that are observable, measurable, and changeable.

Managers are concerned with attitude because they see or hear an individual's unacceptable actions and behavior and assume that the source of that behavior resides in the individual's attitude. "If I could change her attitude," they tell themselves, "then she wouldn't act that way."

Their error involves making the assumption that an attitudinal deficiency is the cause of the unacceptable behavior rather than dealing with the directly observable behavior itself. It is useful to think about the relationship between attitudes and actions as a circle (see Figure 3-1).

Certainly the individual's attitude—that potpourri of hopes, dreams, fears, early childhood experiences, genetic makeup, parental influences, and all the other entities and circumstances that make

Figure 3-1. The attitude/action circle.

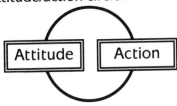

up the inner world of each of us—influences our behavior, the things we say and do. But it is equally true that our actions—our specific, observable, measurable behavior—influence how we feel about ourselves and the world around us.

As managers, our legitimate concern is with the things the person chooses to do, not with what is going on in that individual's mind. We have no right to try to get inside the head of the subordinate, lifting up the rugs of the psyche to see what will come crawling out. All kinds of things may come crawling out, none of which is any of our business. We do, however, have not only the right but also the responsibility to be concerned with the actions and conduct and deportment of the individual.

In a recent seminar at a large hospital in the Southwest, the director of the dietary department began the problem identification process by describing an individual who she claimed had a bad attitude. "How do you know?" I asked her.

"He's not a team player," she responded.

The whole seminar group and I then analyzed what had just happened. To support one generalization—"He has an attitude problem"—she had simply offered up another—"He's not a team player."

"Let me try a different approach," I responded, once she and the others saw how common it is to try to support one judgment or generalization by offering up another. "If you had to prove in court that this person truly did have a lousy attitude, what could you offer as evidence?"

I divided the group in two. I asked the dietary director and her teammates to come up with a list of the actual things that an individual might do that would be acceptable evidence that the person really did have a problem with working effectively as a team member. The other half of the group I set to work generating a list of actions that they would accept as specific evidence that an individual was indeed a team player.

Their results:

Actual Performance
(evidence that someone is not a team player)

- Works on obviously low-priority job tasks when she could be assisting others with much more important parts of the job.

- Wanders in other areas with no valid reason.
- Does only those tasks that are specifically assigned.
- Says "That's not my job" when asked to take charge of an unusual situation.
- Makes negative comments about the quality of others' suggestions (for example, "That's a dopey idea").
- Makes negative comments about other people (for example, "What doofus here is trying to say is . . ." when a fellow worker got tongue-tied during a team meeting).
- Makes no effort to get along with others (for example, sits alone in the cafeteria at lunch, doesn't participate in group social activities, and says, "I don't need anyone's help" when the manager asks a fellow employee to work with her on a minor project).

Desired Performance
(evidence that someone is a team player)

- Demonstrates a spirit of cooperation (for example, doesn't monopolize time during a team meeting).
- Offers up solutions to team problems and not just complaints about their existence.
- Supports co-workers' ideas and suggestions.
- Offers to assist others in their duties when time is available.
- Supports co-workers by making positive statements about them and asking if they need help.
- Asks co-workers for assistance in her projects to demonstrate that others are also members of the team.
- Assists others when they ask for help.

The best way to overcome the temptation to generalize or be judgmental about problems is to ask the question, What do I know for sure? You never know for sure that an individual has an attitudinal deficiency; you do know for sure the visible, measurable, and unarguable behavioral manifestations of the internal problem, whatever it may be.

Determining the Cause

Once we have clearly identified the specific change necessary in an individual's performance, the next step is to determine why the employee isn't doing the job properly right now.

When a person isn't performing the way we expect, there are only two causes: either a deficiency in knowledge or a deficiency in execution. Either he doesn't know how to do the job right, or he does know how to do it right but something is getting in the way. The easiest way to determine the actual cause is to ask the question, Could he do the job properly if his life depended on it?

If the answer is no—that is, no matter how hard he tried or how motivated he might be, he couldn't do the job right—then we're probably looking at a problem caused by a deficiency in knowledge. The individual doesn't have the knowledge or skills required to do the job right, and some kind of training is probably required.

But if the answer is yes—he could do the job properly if he had to, but he still isn't performing properly—then we're dealing with a deficiency in execution. In this case, the employee has the knowledge and skills required, but still isn't meeting expectations.

It's important to distinguish between knowledge and execution problems because the solutions will be very different. Training is the obvious solution to a knowledge problem, but training won't help when the cause of the problem is an execution deficiency.

When discussing performance deficiencies on their subordinate's part, managers often err by describing them as training problems. If we define performance problems as training problems, we are confusing the cause of the problem with its solution. We are committing the same error as the individual who goes to the doctor with a headache and says, "Doc, I've got an aspirin problem." He doesn't have an aspirin problem; he has a headache. Aspirin may be a solution. Antibiotics may be a solution. Brain surgery may be a solution. But his problem isn't aspirin—the problem is, his head hurts. The manager doesn't have a training problem, he has a performance deficiency.

Training may occasionally be the solution to performance problems, but the experience of several thousand managers with whom I have worked suggests that it rarely is. Hundreds of times I have asked managers to make lists of the specific performance problems they face. They write down the things their subordinates are doing that need to be changed. We refine them into detailed and measurable statements of desired behavior and actual behavior.

Once they have written their statements in terms that are specific and unarguable, I ask them to determine whether each of the problems that they have identified is a knowledge issue or an execution issue. Is this one caused by a lack of knowledge and skill, or is this situation one where the individual could be performing properly if he had to, but isn't?

The results are always the same. Out of two dozen problems, perhaps one or two will be caused by a deficiency in knowledge. Another two or three may represent a combination of the two. But by far the great majority are issues where the deficiency is one of execution. The individual could be doing the job right if he had to. He does know how, they tell me, but he isn't executing.

Recognize the limitations of training. To be blunt, the only thing that training can predictably do is provide knowledge and skills where they don't already exist. As valuable as this may be, most of the time it takes something other than training to solve the performance problems managers face.

Solving Execution Problems

Deficiencies in knowledge are cured by training. What do you do, however, when the person knows how to perform properly but still isn't doing the job right?

These are the cases where managers are particularly inclined to blame the employee's bad attitude or complain that he just doesn't care. While in some cases it may turn out that the individual truly does not care, usually the problem results from something interfering with proper performance. The need here is not for training; it is for job engineering. Three strategies are available to put things right: (1) removing job interferences, (2) providing performance feedback, and (3) arranging appropriate consequences.

Removing Job Interferences

We can expect people to perform their jobs well only if they have all the resources required to do the job properly. If a person does not have the equipment needed to do a job or receives conflicting instructions, or if a bad environment or poor working conditions interfere with job performance, the employee will be unable to do the job right.

Job interferences are frequently difficult to identify since we may be so used to going around them that we don't even notice that they exist. It is often useful simply to ask if there's anything that gets in people's way as they try to perform successfully.

In today's business environment, no organization is able to provide all of the resources that would enable every employee to do his job without interferences. Limited resources are, and will continue to be, a fact of life. Too often, however, the obstacles that interfere with job performance are ones that could be easily eliminated if the manager actively seeks to help his employees perform well.

Providing Performance Feedback

A recent survey reported that fully 80 percent of American men believe that they are in the top 10 percent of athletic ability for their age group. In the absence of accurate feedback, people tend to believe that they are better than they truly are.

Regular, accurate, and timely information is one of the most important tools for any individual to use in maintaining acceptable job performance.

The classic application of using performance feedback to improve job performance involved Emery Air Freight's success in increasing the use of containers to consolidate several small packages into one large container. The company's stated goal was 95 percent utilization of containers and, while achievement was not precisely measured, the assumption on the part of most managers and employees was that the 95 percent goal was being achieved regularly.

One day Ed Feeney, an Emery senior manager, actually audited the operation to see what percentage of shipments that could be containerized actually were. He was astounded at the result. Instead of 95 percent, it was 45 percent.

The problem was corrected by providing feedback to each individual dock worker about his actual level of performance. This was accomplished with a form that required the dock worker to write the name of the shipper for each item, to note whether or not each package being processed met the requirements to be containerized, and to indicate whether or not it actually was containerized. At the end of the shift the dock worker calculated the actual percentage of those containerized against those that should have been containerized, and turned the form over to his foreman. When this form was introduced nationwide the overnight result was an increase in containerization from a national average of 45 percent to 95 percent.[1]

Arranging Appropriate Consequences

When people are punished for doing their jobs well, or rewarded for doing them poorly, or discover that it makes no difference how well or poorly they perform, problems invariably result.

Several years ago I was asked by Ted Hattan, United Air Lines' director of reservations, to create a training program for the company's experienced reservations agents. We met in his office to talk about what he wanted the program to accomplish.

The problem, he explained, was not at all one of courtesy or customer service. They regularly monitored calls and knew that the agents, almost without exception, were doing an excellent job of providing information and booking flights. The difficulty, Hattan explained, was that they weren't selling. "A secretary calls and tells the agent that her boss and three of his people are planning to fly next Wednesday from Washington to San Francisco and asks what time our flights leave. That's a perfect selling situation. But all the agent does is tell her what times our flights to San Francisco leave then thanks her for calling and hangs up. No effort to sell at all . . . a blown opportunity. I need you to teach them to sell!"

Before beginning work on an advanced selling skills program, I asked Hattan to let me talk to some of the agents and supervisors. It didn't take long to discover that a training program would have been worthless.

United's reservations office was a huge room on the second floor of the hangar. Over 250 agents sat in rows, each one wired to her phone and computer. High on the wall, about 15 inches across, was a red light that looked like a giant taillight from an ugly 1950s sedan. Whenever customers were calling and the office was so busy

1. Ferdinand F. Fournies, *Coaching for Improved Work Performance* (New York: Van Nostrand Reinhold, 1978), p. 103.

that the calls went into the holding queue, the red light would flash like a monstrous turn signal. The supervisors would then scurry up and down the aisles, whispering to the agents, "Take more calls. . . . We're holding calls. . . . Take more calls!" The agents would then simply provide information and abandon any attempt to sell.

A second problem emerged. Ask an agent how he or she was doing as far as sales were concerned and the response would be, "Just fine." Although everyone knew that the office stressed selling, nobody had any specific information on his or her actual sales. They all thought that if there were problems with insufficient selling, somebody else wasn't trying hard enough.

Finally I learned the biggest problem of all. While Ted Hattan and his managers talked constantly about the importance of selling, the only data they measured and fed back to the agents were "calls per hour." Calls per hour was the measurement used to evaluate performance when appraisal time came around; calls per hour determined the amount of an agent's merit increase. When that secretary called in asking about flight times, the sophisticated agent would quickly review the schedule and then graciously say, "Thank you for calling United." Hey, a call's a call.

The solution to Ted Hattan's problem was simple, cheap, and elegant. One third of the agents were shown how to tap the computer to find out exactly what their sales for the day or week had been and how they compared to the office average. They were told to stay with a sales opportunity even when the call-holding light was flashing. And they were told that while calls per hour was important, turning nibbles into actual seats booked was much more important and that their performance appraisals would reflect both measures. They were also given a refresher training session on how to convert inquiries into seats sold.

Another third of the office got the same adjustment—computer feedback, rearranged consequences—but no training. The final third of the office was a control group. They experienced no changes.

The results were both predictable and surprising. It was predictable that the first two groups would far outperform the third, and they did. What was surprising was that there was no significant difference between the improved performance of the group that got feedback, consequences, and training and the other group that received only the job engineering changes. Both increased sales about

24 percent. The other surprise was that there was very little reduction on either of the "experimental groups" in their calls per hour. Agents monitored their conversations carefully, responding to informational calls quickly and sticking with nibbles until the sale was made.

Few performance problems are caused by an employee's lack of knowledge or skill. Training is the answer to deficiencies in knowledge, but when reasonably experienced performers fail to perform properly, a lack of knowledge is rarely the cause.

Some performance problems are caused by position mismatches: the square peg in the round hole. Neither training nor job engineering nor disciplinary action can cure these situations. Transfer if possible, downgrade to a position the person can handle if not.

The solution to a great many performance deficiencies, however, lies in reengineering the job. Arrange for people to get feedback so that they know exactly how well or poorly they are doing, remove any obstacles that thwart good performance, rearrange the consequences so that performing well makes a difference.

A Shift in Responsibility

Until the alternatives of training and job engineering have been tried and failed or, as in the case of theft or assault, when they are obviously inappropriate, the Discipline Without Punishment approach assumes that the responsibility for finding a solution to the problem remains with the manager and the organization and not with the individual. This assumption is a useful one to make. First, it is frequently accurate. Problems that arise in organizations often are caused more by organizational deficiencies than by personal failings.

Second, if the problem is not solved early on by training and job engineering, the efforts to find a solution will obviously continue. Later approaches will involve more serious discussions with the employee, including formal disciplinary transactions. If the problem still remains uncorrected, termination will finally result. But at some point in the process—perhaps when the manager is reviewing the action he has taken so far in order to gain approval for a more serious step; perhaps after the individual's termination when a judge or arbitrator is reviewing the case; or perhaps during a sleepless night just before he wields the ax of termination—the question will arise, Did the company, did the manager, do all that could be done to solve the problem?

Investing time in the earliest stages will allow that nettlesome question to be answered comfortably and sufficiently. No longer will the manager, the night before he fires a subordinate, have to grapple with the question, Is there anything else I could have done?

The answer to that question is no. There are things that the manager and the organization must do before saying that the responsibility for correcting the situation now lies entirely with the individual. The manager must make sure that the job can be done as expected by a normal person with normal training. The manager must make sure that the employee has had the training needed to perform properly. The manager must be sure that the employee knows exactly what the company's expectations are and how he's doing with respect to them. Finally, within the limits of organizational realities and constraints, the manager must make sure that no problems with obstacles, feedback, or inappropriate consequences prevent the person from doing the job right.

But once the manager can state that the employee knows exactly what is expected, that she is recognized appropriately when she performs as expected, that she knows how to do the job properly, encounters no obstacles, and knows exactly how well or how poorly she is doing, the manager has done all that he can reasonably be asked to do. It is at this point that the burden of responsibility shifts from the organization to the employee. The individual with the problem now becomes the one who is fully responsible for its solution.

Part Two
Coaching

Coaching

Before the Meeting:
1. Determine DESIRED and ACTUAL performance
2. Determine the GOOD BUSINESS REASONS why the problem must be solved
3. Determine the LOGICAL CONSEQUENCES if the problem continues
4. Determine the appropriate ACTION STEP

During the Meeting:
1. Confirm that the planned ACTION IS APPROPRIATE
2. Gain the employee's AGREEMENT TO CHANGE
3. DETERMINE THE ACTION the employee will take

After the Meeting:
1. DOCUMENT the discussion
2. FOLLOW UP to make sure that the problem has been solved

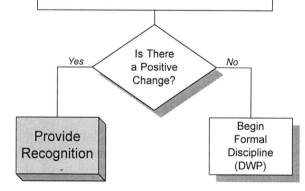

Is There a Positive Change?

Yes → Provide Recognition

No → Begin Formal Discipline (DWP)

4

Preparing for a Coaching Session

The process of solving people problems so that problems are eliminated and relationships are enhanced begins with coaching.

What Coaching Is and Isn't

A coaching session is a serious and planned discussion between a manager and an employee about the need to correct a problem and improve performance. It has specific goals and follows a definite structure. Unlike impulsive or spontaneous casual discussions about problems, a coaching session always involves careful planning in advance.

It is useful to distinguish between three kinds of discussions supervisors regularly hold with subordinates: casual conversations, coaching sessions, and disciplinary transactions. Most managers assume that casual conversations and coaching sessions are very much alike, that disciplinary transactions are significantly different.

Because they believe that casual conversations and coaching sessions are similar while disciplinary transactions are very different, managers are less effective in both their coaching sessions and their disciplinary transactions. Since they consider casual conversations and coaching sessions as virtually synonymous and indistinguishable, they put as little effort into a coaching session as they do into the hundreds of routine and ordinary conversations they have with subordinates every day of their work lives. They follow no planned structure when they hold what they feel is a coaching session, believing that such things as structure, seriousness, and formality are reserved for those nasty transactions called "discipline."

Even worse, since they know that a disciplinary transaction is a serious piece of corporate business, they usually assume that the appropriate tone for this unpleasant discussion should be cold, unfeeling, and detached. They then adopt a personal demeanor either reserved and aloof or harsh and indignant.

Managers act this way because they mistakenly believe that disciplinary action represents the steps they must take when they have decided to discharge a subordinate. Since terminating the individual is rarely their goal when a problem first arises, they often conduct an excessive number of informal discussions and "coaching 'n' counseling" transactions, alternately friendly and stern, but never planned, structured, and well thought out. They continue these casual and undocumented discussions long past the point at which they have any predictable chance of success, since they believe that once they put their toe into the arena of formal disciplinary action they must proceed, in lockstep, all the way down the path to termination.

Actually, under the Discipline Without Punishment system, coaching conversations and disciplinary transactions are almost indistinguishable. The only significant difference between coaching sessions and disciplinary transactions is that in a disciplinary transaction, the supervisor advises the employee that the discussion they are having is a formal level of the Discipline Without Punishment system and then documents the discussion following the conversation.

The steps that the supervisor follows for an effective Coaching Session are identical to those of an effective disciplinary conversation. Before the meeting, he identifies the specific problem that needs to be solved and analyzes why a change must be made. Then he discusses it with the employee to gain the individual's agreement. After the meeting, he documents what they have discussed and then follows up to make sure the problem has been corrected. The appropriate tone throughout the process is calm, dignified, respectful, businesslike, and professional, whether the discussion is a first coaching session or a Decision Making Leave.

Coaching sessions are far more similar to disciplinary discussions than they are to informal casual conversations. Coaching sessions and disciplinary discussions are both systematic (planned, structured, goal oriented) and professional (dignified, polite, courteous). The sooner managers understand this, the more effective both transactions will be at solving problems and enhancing relationships.

The Process of Coaching

The process of coaching in Discipline Without Punishment involves three components: those things the manager does before the meeting to prepare for the face-to-face session; the coaching discussion itself; and the things the manager does when the meeting is over and the employee returns to work.

This chapter will cover the first component, the manager's pre-meeting preparation. The three essential items of preparation are

1. Determining the category the problem falls into
2. Identifying the specific difference between actual and desired performance
3. Analyzing why it is important that the problem be solved

The next chapter, "Conducting the Coaching Discussion," will explain exactly how to hold a discussion about the need for a change in performance. Whether the discussion is one of the formal levels of Discipline Without Punishment or a nondisciplinary transaction, the structure and procedures for the face-to-face discussion will be the same.

The third component of coaching, the things the manager is responsible for once the discussion with the employee has been completed, basically involves documenting the discussion and following up to make sure that the problem has been solved. These responsibilities will be covered in Chapters 6 and 7.

Determining the Category of the Problem

As described in Chapter 3, any performance or behavior problem can be separated into one of three categories: attendance, performance, and conduct.

In preparing for a coaching session, start by determining which of the three types of problems is the primary concern. While an individual may have a need for improvement in several areas (an unacceptable attendance record may be combined with a failure to submit scheduled progress reports on time), keeping unrelated issues separated increases the chances of getting each problem solved. In other words: Got two problems? Hold two discussions.

At early stages, when the probability of correction and commitment are highest, there is no absolute prohibition against talking about several performance concerns in one informal conversation. But when a manager's concern has grown to the point where the manager has decided to schedule a specific meeting with the subordinate to discuss the need for change, restricting the discussion to the issue of primary concern will increase the odds that the subordinate will agree to change and return to fully acceptable performance. Dumping a gunnysack of problems will suggest to the individual that the real issue is not his own poor performance but some unrelated discontent on the manager's part. The subordinate will discount all of the unconnected deficiencies about which the manager is complaining as merely additional proof of the manager's tendency to nitpick and relieve pressure by taking out his frustrations on his subordinates. Quick and unconvincing agreement will probably be forthcoming, as the subordinate, eager to get the meeting over with and get back to the job at hand, simply concurs and harmonizes with whatever the boss puts forth.

Managers can increase their effectiveness by starting a meeting with a multitroubled subordinate by saying, "Jack, there are probably a number of things that we should be talking about. In the last few weeks I've expressed my concern at various times about the number of customer contacts you're making, about your reluctance to get involved with the trade association to make new contacts, even about your being away from your desk too often to catch a smoke. But those things are really secondary. Today I want to concentrate on talking about one key issue with you. That is, your total sales have fallen by 16 percent in the last three months. . . ."

Now the subordinate knows that while all those other infractions have not been forgotten, they are secondary. The manager can concentrate on the most significant issue and then, once agreement to solve the critical problem has been gained, can mention the need for a total commitment to acceptable performance as the meeting is wrapping up.

It is easy to determine the category into which a problem falls. Being specific about desired and actual performance is far more difficult.

Determining Actual and Expected Performance

Instead of concentrating on the precise change needed in the subordinate's performance most managers talk in vague and general terms. Since the manager himself has not taken the time to determine exactly what acceptable performance is—and what it is not—it is almost impossible for the subordinate to know exactly what is expected.

Why is it so important to be so specific? Consider what happens in a restaurant when we experience an evening of enjoyable food but wretched service. To communicate our displeasure with the waiter's service, we leave a minuscule tip. When the waiter discovers our meager tip, our unhappiness will instantly be communicated. But in the absence of any data about the cause of our unhappiness, the waiter's immediate assumption will be that the problem resides not with the service he provided but with us as the customer.

Consider all the explanations the waiter is likely to come up with to explain the insulting tip:

- The customer made a mistake—the tiny tip was inadvertent.
- There was something wrong with the food.
- There was something wrong with the restaurant—too warm, too cold, too smoky.
- The customer had run out of money and left everything that he had.

In each case, the waiter's explanation of the lousy tip acknowledged the fact that a problem existed but denied the possibility that he himself was the cause. The waiter will tell himself that whatever the reason may be for the meager tip, it certainly had nothing to do with poor service.

The same situation happens in organizations when managers

fail to be specific about the problem and the solution required. If the manager communicates only a general feeling of unhappiness, the subordinate will understand how he feels but will explain it away in the same way the waiter did:

- He's picking on me because his boss chewed him out this morning.
- She's disappointed that she didn't get appointed to the steering committee.
- He must have had a fight with his wife.
- She's one day away from vacation and is just trying to get us all to work hard while she's gone.
- He just doesn't like us elderly, black, female, Spanish-surnamed, handicapped homosexuals.
- It must be her time of the month.

To solve problems effectively we must be able to describe what it is that we want and what it is that we get in the individual's performance. It is the subordinate's responsibility to close the gap between expected and actual performance. Our responsibility is to specify exactly what the gap is.

For some problems, it's easy. Problems that fall into the attendance category are the easiest to identify specifically, because the gap between expected and actual performance is always clear: "Between June 16 and July 23, Jane Edmondson was absent from work on three occasions for a total of five days. In that same period she reported to work late by more than ten minutes on two separate occasions."

Note that the problem statement says nothing about the cause of Jane's absence. It does not say that Jane was ill or called in sick or abused her sick-leave privileges or did anything other than simply fail to report to work every day on time. That is all that the manager knows for sure. The cause of Jane's absences may be considered at some other more appropriate time. But at this point, when our only task is to identify the difference between desired and actual performance, we restrict ourselves to writing down the answers to two straightforward questions:

1. What is the expected performance? (What do I want?)
2. What is the actual performance? (What do I get?)

Here are some examples of various problems stated in terms of actual and expected performance:

Expected Performance: Employees are to smoke only in designated smoking areas or outside the building.
Actual Performance: George Adamson was seen smoking in the cafeteria.

Expected Performance: Upon being given an instruction by any member of management, employees are to perform the task assigned. If they believe that the manager giving the instruction is in error, they are to complete the task assigned and then question the appropriateness of the assignment.
Actual Performance: Upon being told by the department manager to stop what she was doing and assist two other employees to finish a complicated customer order, Julie Sonnenberg stated, "You're not my boss. You can't tell me what to do." She continued to work at the task she had been assigned earlier by her immediate supervisor.

Expected Performance: All drivers are expected to operate their vehicles courteously.
Actual Performance: On May 17 a woman called the 800 number posted on the back of company trucks to complain about the erratic driving and speeding of a company truck that was being driven at the time by Danny Di Sabatino.

Expected Performance: All nurses are expected to respond to any patient call button within three minutes on the 11 P.M. to 7 A.M. shift.
Actual Performance: On the evening of March 16, patient Claudia Gonzales complained to the day charge nurse that the night nurse hadn't responded to her call button the night before.

Expected Performance: All employees of the corporation are prohibited from engaging in any unwanted or inappropriate behavior of a sexual nature, whether physical, verbal, nonverbal, or any other type, expressed toward any employee, customer, applicant, ven-

	dor, supplier, or other individual having a rela-tionship with the organization.
Actual *Performance:*	On September 5, Joe McKenna approached Sharon Peterman at the copy machine and said, "You sure make that sweater look good." When Peterman turned away without responding, Mc-Kenna said, "The package sure is pretty. . . . I'd sure like to get my hands on the contents."

Making Clear, Unambiguous Statements

In each of the above cases, there are several common factors. While the problems themselves are completely unrelated, the statements of expected and actual performance are clear and unambiguous. Not one contains any statement that involves a judgment by the manager or a generalization based on the facts. Instead, the statement simply provides a clear description of the variance between what was expected and what was delivered.

The statements, in other words, are written to be *unarguable*. The individual certainly may protest that he really had good reasons for failing to meet the performance expectation, or may say that the seriousness of the action is being exaggerated, or may argue that failing to meet the expectation is not a serious matter. While these issues may be worth discussing, there is no argument that the actual description of the employee's action is accurate. Adamson was, in fact, observed smoking. Mrs. Gonzales did, in fact, complain about a delay in getting a response to her call button. Julie Sonnenberg did, in fact, refuse to follow the department manager's instruction.

Note also that there is no indication of the seriousness of the problem in any of the statements. In these five examples we have illustrations of five unrelated problems that can arise in any organization. The least serious may be George Adamson's decision to smoke in the cafeteria. A word in George's ear will probably snuff out that situation forever.

More serious is the example of the night nurse's failure to re-spond to a patient call button. The statement of desired performance expresses a clearly defined performance expectation: respond to all call buttons within three minutes. Failure to meet the standard may result in an extremely serious consequence (if the patient was calling because of a life-threatening incident) or may be completely trivial (if the reason for the call was the patient's desire for a kind word and a back rub). But the effects of her failure to perform is not our concern yet. The issue at this stage in the process is to describe exactly what the desired performance is and exactly how the individual failed to meet that requirement.

George Adamson's smoking problem may be dealt with simply by saying, "Come on, George . . . you know you can't light up here." The more serious problem with the nurse's failure to respond to a call button requires anything from a casual and informal reminder (if the patient is a known crank), to a very serious disciplinary transaction (if the nurse consciously ignored the summons and the safety of the patient was compromised). Finally, the sexual harassment charge, if proved, could even result in the termination of the harasser, based on the complete set of facts that will emerge during the investigation. But at this first step of the coaching procedure, we will go no further than to identify precisely what the variance is between what we want and what we get.

Avoiding Assumptions

In none of the descriptions of actual and expected performance are there any assumptions or characterizations or attitudinal allegations. In the most serious example, the situation involving an apparent sexual harassment case involving Joe McKenna and Sharon Peterman, the description of expected performance is simply the corporation's published policy regarding sexual harassment. In the description of actual performance, the statement does not say that McKenna harassed Peterman. There are no characterizations of his behavior as leering or ogling. It does not say that he made his statements suggestively or lewdly or in a vulgar manner. It does not claim that he was obscene or vulgar or carnal or lascivious or lecherous, since these would be conclusions drawn on the basis of what was actually done, and since they speak to McKenna's presumed intent or purpose, would be very hard to support if challenged. Instead, the statement simply describes exactly what he said and did without embellishment. He walked up to her in this place, spoke these words, and when she turned away without responding, spoke these additional words. The statement is not only unambiguous, it is unarguable.

In the above case, McKenna may argue that his remarks were misinterpreted. He may claim that this was part of an ongoing relationship they had and that he assumed that they would be taken in the light and playful manner he intended them. He may present all kinds of arguments in his defense, but the unarguable fact is that these were the words that he spoke. That is what we know for sure.

Determining the Facts

What do we know for sure? In preparing for a coaching session with an employee, this is the single most important question we can ask ourselves. We do not know that McKenna harassed Peterman. It sounds like a blatant example of sexual harassment, and later it may be determined that it is. At this point, however, all we know for sure is that he spoke these words and she complained about it.

We do not know for sure whether the night nurse had a good reason for not meeting the three-minute standard for responding to call buttons. She may have been involved in a critical care situation elsewhere on the floor. We do not know for sure whether Julie Sonnenberg had a justifiable reason for not following the department head's instructions. We do know for sure that she refused.

The point is not to turn managers into prosecuting attorneys, but to force managers to restrict themselves to dealing only with information that no defense attorney could twist and use against the manager later. By restricting ourselves only to what we know for sure, we will be far more comfortable when we talk to the employee about the need to change. We accuse the employee of nothing. We make no assumptions about the individual's intentions or motives. We cast no aspersions on the truthfulness of any statements the employee makes in his defense. We are simply saying, "Here is what we expect, and here is what actually happened. There is a difference, and this difference must be corrected."

This approach also makes it easier for managers to confront problems when the information they must deal with is secondhand. In two of the examples above, the situations with the night nurse and the truck driver who was reported to be driving erratically and speeding, neither the individual's direct supervisor nor any other member of management observed the inappropriate behavior. Managers are often reluctant to confront this kind of problem, anticipating that the employee's reaction will be, "How do you know what I did? You weren't there!"

In these cases, dealing exclusively with what the manager knows for sure allows him to confront the problem more confidently and more accurately. In the case of the nurse, the nursing supervisor can comfortably respond to the employee's rebuttal, "Barbara, you're right. I wasn't there and therefore I don't know all the details of what happened and why. What I do know is that when I came in to work this morning I received a complaint from a very upset patient who told me that she had rung her call button twice during the night. Once, she said, there had been no response. She said that half an hour later she rang the button again and you showed up about ten minutes after that. I don't know whether she is correct or not. What I do know is that I got a serious complaint, and that's what we need to talk about. How do you need to manage your response to call buttons so that we never get any complaints?"

Likewise, in the driving situation, it is far easier to deal with the situation and get a problem solved (if, in fact, a problem actually does exist) if the manager acknowledges up front what the employee already knows and is eager to point out—that the manager was not there and therefore has no accurate data about the way in which the employee was driving his truck. But that is not the issue, the manager can explain to the individual. "Granted," the manager can say to Danny, "it is conceivable that the woman who called to complain about your driving is a nut case. She sounded entirely reasonable and rational on the phone when I talked to her, but it is possible that she may be deranged. But that doesn't address the issue that someone who observed your driving was sufficiently concerned to take the time to call the company to bring it to our attention. That is all we know for sure, and that is what we need to talk about. What do you need to do in the future, Danny, to make sure that your driving never provokes people into feeling that they need to call us about it?"

Danny, the driver, may well come back with a rejoinder about being unfairly accused, arguing that he is invariably a model driver. But his boss is in a strong position to press for a commitment for a performance change, based not on the supposition that Danny's driving was excessively fast and erratic (which it probably was, but the manager does not know for sure) but on the fact that, whatever his driving demeanor was, it was of such a nature that it caused someone to call and complain.

"I'm not asking you to slow down and drive safely," Danny's boss can tell him, "because you have told me that you already are and I believe that you are telling me the truth. What I am asking for is your agreement that, whatever it takes, you will drive in such a manner that no one ever feels the need to call us and complain."

When the manager has identified the problem in terms of the specific difference between actual and expected performance so that the description is *unarguable*, the second part of the manager's premeeting preparation has been completed. He knows the category the problem falls into, and he knows the exact difference between desired performance and actual.

But the manager is not yet ready to initiate a discussion. Merely being aware of the existence of a problem is insufficient ammunition to generate a commitment to change. Now that we know exactly what the problem is, we must also be prepared to explain why it must be solved. That is the final part of our premeeting preparation.

The Purpose of the Discussion

When a manager and a subordinate sit down to talk about a problem, what is the manager's goal for that conversation?

The easy and obvious answer is, of course, to get the problem solved. And while solving the problem is the long-term goal, the actual correction will not occur until some point in the future, long after the meeting is over. The question I am raising here is a more tightly focused one: What needs to happen while the meeting is going on to tell the manager that he can say, "Ahhhhhh, now I have achieved my goal. Now I can wrap this conversation up and we can get back to work."

What is your goal during the meeting itself? What needs to happen while you and the subordinate are talking to tell you that you can now bring things to a close because you have accomplished your objective?

It has nothing to do with the manager's feelings about whether the subordinate has sufficiently internalized the necessity for change or fully comprehended the gravity of the situation. It is far, far simpler.

The goal of the meeting is to get the subordinate to agree to change.

That's it. Period.

"Well, that's simple," most managers would respond. "I knew that."

I would then counter with a second question: Why is it so important to get the employee to agree to change?

The obvious answer seems to be that if he says he'll change then he probably will. Certainly the individual who agrees to change is more likely to actually change and get back to fulfilling the requirements of the job than is the person who is simply ordered to. But there is a more subtle and more powerful reason.

Have you ever experienced roller-coaster performance? Have you ever had someone working for you who had some performance problems and got better for a while after you talked to him but then reverted back to the unacceptable level after a while? And you'd talk again and he'd get better for a while and then slough off again? And you'd talk again, and the cycle would continue: talk, get better, get worse; talk, get better, get worse.

Most managers are familiar with that scenario.

Here's the antidote. The reason that the goal of the conversation is to get the employee to agree to change is not only because the person who agrees to change is more likely to change. The other, more important reason is this: If the person agrees to correct a problem and then later the same problem arises again, the manager will hold another conversation with the individual. But the subject of this second conversation will be different from that of the first. This time the subject will be the employee's failure to live up to the agreement.

In this second conversation, the manager might say something like this: "George, a week or so ago we talked about the need for you to smoke only in the prescribed areas or outside. You agreed that you would do so. This morning I noticed that you were again smoking in the cafeteria. But I'm less concerned about your continuing to smoke in a restricted area than I am about your decision not to live up to your agreement. That's the real issue now. Tell me, George, how can we maintain an employment relationship with someone who decides not to live up to an agreement that he makes with his boss?"

Now *there* is a question worth asking.

Gaining the employee's agreement serves two important purposes. First, if the manager is successful in getting the individual to agree to perform at the level of expected performance, the odds go up that the individual will in fact live up to the agreement that he has made.

But the second reason is the manager's ace in the hole. If the misconduct or unacceptable performance continues, the subsequent conversation will focus not just on the continuation of the original problem, but on the employee's failure to live up to the agreement.

Gaining Agreement

How do we gain a person's agreement?

The work we did in identifying the specific difference between actual and desired performance makes the process of gaining agreement far easier than it might otherwise be. Since we know exactly what we want, and since what we want represents nothing more than what the individual is being paid to do, we start by describing the problem and asking for agreement.

Most of the folks, most of the time, when approached by a manager calmly and professionally and asked to agree to do what they are getting paid to do, will agree. Will they live up to the agreement? We don't know, but we can never know during the meeting. All we can do during the meeting is gain the employee's agreement to change, secure in the knowledge that the odds are great that once a person agrees to solve a problem he will do so.

But let's say he doesn't. Let's say that George's response to our reasonable request that he agree to smoke only in designated areas is not agreement but objection.

"Oh, come on," George responds. "It's no big deal. I always ask the people around me if it's OK before I light up. If anybody ever says anything to me I put it right out. I waste a lot of time walking downstairs to the designated area and that's time taken away from my work. You used to smoke, too, you know. And you weren't as careful about lighting up around other people as I am. And look at the prez—he smokes anywhere he wants. Don't the rules apply to everybody? Just because he owns the joint, does that mean he doesn't have to follow the rules he makes for us grunts? Why are you making such a big deal about such a little thing. . . . Don't you have anything more important to do?"

When managers are slammed with a salvo like that in response to an apparently simple request that a rule be followed, they usually respond in one of two unproductive ways. They may back off apologetically, since many of the things that George said are true (the president doesn't always model the behavior he asks of others; you used to be a smoker yourself; George is actually quite solicitous of others before he lights up). On the other hand, they don their traditional armor of power and authority and respond to George: "I'm the boss, it's a rule, you'll do as you're told!" Managers who react that way are typically following this line of reasoning: The fact is, I *am* the boss. The fact is, it *is* a rule. If George doesn't like it, let him work somewhere else where the rules are different!

To those managers, I would point out the obvious: Yes, you are the boss—you've got power. Yes, it is a rule—you've got authority. But do power and authority help you solve this problem and enhance your relationship with George? Do power and authority work?

Most managers will admit that having power and authority doesn't always give them the results they want, particularly if the results they seek involve more than mere compliance. The use of power can produce compliance, but commitment cannot be developed through authoritarian means.

Instead of power and authority, a more effective tactic is to seek agreement through considering the good business reasons why the problem must be solved and the logical consequences the employee will face if it is not.

Why is it important that a problem be solved? Why is it important that an individual agree to change once the existence of a problem has been brought to his attention? There must be good business reasons that caused the company to make the rule or create the expectation in the first place.

For George's problem of smoking in restricted areas, simply ask yourself, What are the good business reasons why we don't allow smoking anywhere but in designated areas and outdoors? What difference does it make if someone smokes anyplace he chooses?

A list of good business reasons usually flows forth without difficulty:

- The smell of smoke is offensive to most people.
- Breathing smoke is considered by some authorities to be a health hazard.
- Cigarette smoke, over time, interferes with the heating/venting/air conditioning system, thereby increasing costs.
- The presence of smoke in the workplace is distracting to others and causes them to complain or be distracted from what they are doing.
- Seeing George smoke in a restricted area without consequence is likely to suggest to others that the rules are there for appearance's sake only. Others are likely to start lighting up wherever they please.
- Many of the places in which smoking is restricted are off-limits for safety reasons as well as the comfort and convenience of others. If George smokes in these areas he may be creating a safety hazard.

Two objectives are achieved by creating a list of good business reasons why it is important that the rule be obeyed and that the problem be solved. First, it increases the confidence of the manager in initiating the discussion. Once the manager has developed this list, he knows that the issue is not a trivial concern or merely a whim. There are substantive and important reasons why the rule or performance expectation exists.

Second, having a list of good business reasons why a problem must be solved increases the probability that the manager will be successful in gaining the subordinate's agreement to solve the problem and return to fully acceptable performance.

Most people will agree to solve a problem if it is brought to their attention in a mature, professional, and businesslike way: "George, I have a problem. The company's smoking regulations provide that employees may smoke only in designated areas or outside the building, but I noticed this morning that you were smoking in the cafeteria. I need for you to agree that you'll restrict your smoking only to the appropriate areas from now on."

It would be difficult for George to refuse to agree if that statement were made to him in a serious and businesslike way. But as we saw in the example above, George did fail to agree and instead responded that other people, including the president, also smoke in off-limits locations; that he always asked permission before smoking; and that walking from his work area to the smoking area wastes time. Why are you making such a big deal about it? asks George.

With your list of the problem's effects, you can now respond to George's objections confidently. "You're right, George. It does seem to be a minor problem. I can understand why you would think I'm making a mountain out of a molehill. But actually that's not the case. It really is important.

"Here's why," you continue. "When you smoke in an off-limits location it may bother other people, even though they may not complain directly to you. We want our employees to be free of any health risks and, whether you agree with them or not, there are a lot of doctors who say that secondhand smoke is dangerous. Your smoke gets into the ventilation system and increases the frequency of maintenance problems. And even though I have no control over what the president chooses to do, I can control how I work with people in my own unit. That's why I need you to agree to smoke only where it's permitted."

Once again, it would be difficult for George to refuse. His boss has agreed with the fact that it is easy to believe that the smoking issue is a very minor problem. His boss has then explained, calmly and professionally, why smoking is restricted to certain areas. Finally, the boss has closed the discussion by simply asking George to do no more than what he was getting paid to do—to follow the rules of the company.

Determining the Logical Consequences

In rare cases people will refuse to agree to change their behavior even after they are told why their behavior creates a problem. In this case the manager must be prepared to explain the logical consequences of their choice not to do what they are getting paid to do.

In identifying the consequences that someone will face if he continues to perform unacceptably, we are simply advising the individual that the decisions he makes have consequences, as all decisions do. If someone decides that in spite of knowing that what he is doing is a problem (missing deadlines, for example), and in spite of knowing why it's a problem (other people's work is delayed, his own projects get backed up, customers get poor service, managers in other units complain, etc.), he is still going to miss deadlines, there are logical consequences to that decision (like the denial of a merit increase, the refusal to assign the individual to more-important and thus more-satisfying projects, formal disciplinary transactions, closer supervision, etc.).

All decisions have consequences. The logical or natural consequences of an individual's decision to perform well, to exceed the organization's minimum standards, to offer assistance to others when his own work is completed, to speak favorably of the organization with customers and colleagues and outsiders, to invest personal time in developmental activities, will be positive and rewarding.

On the other hand, if a person chooses to do only what he is told to do, to discuss only the negative aspects of life in the enterprise and the failures and shortcomings of his associates, to approach every assignment from the perspective of "What's in it for me?" and never go beyond minimum expectations, the consequences of those decisions will not be nearly as satisfying or rewarding.

Note that the approach just described does not involve the commission of any act for which disciplinary action would be appropriate. The person who chooses to remain just over the line of barely acceptable performance will not be subject to disciplinary action, since the steps of Discipline Without Punishment (or any other discipline system) are appropriate only when specific rules are violated or job performance becomes unacceptable. Maintaining a record of "barely acceptable" will not subject a person to the discipline system; nor will it produce many of the organization rewards enjoyed by those whose commitment is much higher.

Every choice brings consequences. When an individual chooses to perform in a way that the organization finds unacceptable, and the individual chooses to continue that unacceptable behavior even after learning that it is unacceptable and the reasons why, the individual has the right to know what the consequences of that choice are. Certainly they will not be pleasant, but neither will they be threats. They will be straightforward descriptions of the logical, adverse consequences that can be expected when someone decides not to do what he is paid to do.

Generating the Consequences List

In generating the list of natural or logical consequences that are likely to result if the person chooses to continue inappropriate behavior, all managers immediately identify "Further disciplinary action up to and including discharge."

When asked if there are any others, their initial attempts to expand the list usually involve simply restating the initial proposition: "He'll be written up," "She'll be subject to an Oral Reminder," "He will be suspended," "She'll be fired."

While all of these are accurate, all are simply variations on the discipline theme. Are there not others?

Consider an employee who has developed an ongoing problem of doing personal work when she should be working. An informal conversation or two has failed to produce any significant change in her behavior. She still reads magazines and gossips in the break room and chats with her friends on the phone.

Her boss, in getting ready for a formal Coaching Session about the need to do only company business while she is on the clock, has no difficulty in identifying the specific desired and actual performance and in enumerating the good business reasons why personal business must be attended to only on one's own time.

Describing the specifics of the problem itself and the effects of the problem will almost always be sufficient to bring about an agreement from the employee to straighten up and fly right. But if the manager's attempts to gain her agreement to do personal business on her own time are unsuccessful, the manager must be prepared to review the likely consequences that her decision will produce.

Certainly "Further disciplinary action up to and including termination" will be on the list. But there are many other consequences that may turn out to be more powerful. For example:

Manager: Connie, I'm disappointed that you still won't agree to do your personal business only on your own time and only work on company business while you're being paid.

Employee: Yeahbut like I told you, I can't promise that I won't ever get any phone calls. If somebody decides to call me, I can't stop them. And besides, when I'm finished with a big report, I like to take a couple minutes to catch my breath and switch gears for a minute. It's not like I'm spending all day reading novels. Gimme a break, huh?

Manager: Connie, I've told you that doing personal business is a problem and why it's a problem. I need you to agree that you will do only what you're getting paid to do while you're getting paid to do it. If you decide to continue doing personal business, there are consequences to that decision.

Employee: Like what?

Manager: If you decide to keep on doing personal things, that will cause me to decide to move into our discipline process.

Employee: You'd write me up just for taking a phone call?

Manager: The decisions you make affect the decisions that I make. If you decide to continue your personal phone conversations then, yes, I will decide to continue forward with the discipline process. And there are other consequences, too.

Employee: Like what?

Manager: Several things. If you decide not to correct this situation, that will cause me to decide to pay much closer attention to what you're doing. You can expect that I'll be moving you to a desk closer to my office so I can make sure that the problem has disappeared. I'm probably also going to decide not to allow you to participate on the annual event committee that you asked about last week.

Employee: You'd keep me off that committee just because I don't spend every single minute with my nose to the grindstone?

Manager: If you decide not to do what you're getting paid to do, I have no way to justify letting you take time away from your basic job responsibilities. Yes, I would decide that.

Employee: That's not fair.

Manager: What's not fair about that?

Employee: Well, I don't think you should keep me off the committee just because I was reading a magazine or something.

Manager: Connie, the choices you make determine the choices I make. I have no desire to keep you off that committee. But the decision to be on the committee is yours, not mine. If you can agree to do what you're being paid to do and eliminate this problem of doing personal business, then it's easy for me to decide to release you for a special project. If you can't agree to that, then I have no way to justify letting you work on something that is actually less important than your basic job. So it's up to you.

Employee: Well, I really want to do that committee thing.

Manager: So what's your decision?

Employee: I'll do what you want.

Manager: It's not "what I want," Connie. It's what the job requires. The basic job requirement is that you spend your work hours doing your work. I need your agreement that you'll always do that. Can I have it?

Employee: Sure.

Manager: Good. I don't think we're ever going to have to talk about this again, are we?

Employee: No.

Manager: I don't either. Let's get back to work.

In this case the manager was successful in gaining the employee's agreement to change. He got the agreement by reviewing the logical consequences if the employee failed to do what she was being paid to do.

But it is rare that the discussion will ever get to the point where the manager needs to review the list of consequences. Most people do their jobs well and never need any formal coaching about the need to make performance corrections. When problems do arise, most are quickly solved by an informal discussion without any advance preparation.

When a casual conversation fails to solve a problem and the manager moves to a formal coaching session, most of the time he will be successful simply by bringing the existence of the problem to the employee's attention, reviewing the good business reasons why the situation must be resolved, and asking the individual to agree to solve it. So only in rare cases when the employee consistently refuses to agree to change will the manager ever have need to overtly describe the consequences of failure to perform properly. But even though the consequences list is rarely used, generating it increases the manager's self-confidence during the discussion.

The manager's role is to help the individual make wise and rational decisions about job performance by pointing out that both performing well and performing poorly have consequences. Once the employee understands that decisions have consequences, he can make an informed decision to meet the standards of the organization, not because of threats or intimidation but because he understands fully the consequences of both meeting and failing to meet the standards of the organization.

Choosing a Course of Action

Having identified a problem in terms of both its category and the specific expected and actual performance, and having determined both the good business reasons why it must be solved and the consequences the employee will face if it's not, the manager can make a good decision about whether the discussion he will hold will be a nondisciplinary coaching conversation or a formal disciplinary transaction. If a step of the Discipline Without Punishment procedure is appropriate, the analysis the manager has just completed, along with a review of any previous discussions, will indicate which of the formal levels of disciplinary action would be appropriate.

Whether the discussion is a coaching session or a disciplinary transaction, the purpose of the discussion is the same: to get the employee to agree to change, correct the problem, and return to acceptable performance.

5

Conducting the Coaching Discussion

Whether the discussion with the employee is a nondisciplinary coaching session or a formal step of the Discipline Without Punishment system, the goal is the same: to get the employee to agree to solve the problem and return to acceptable performance. By securing the subordinate's agreement to correct the situation, the odds go up that an actual correction will result. If the correction does not follow and the problem continues, the next discussion will concentrate not only on the continuing problem but also on the subordinate's failure to live up to the agreement that he has made.

Before initiating the discussion, it is important to prepare fully, anticipate any difficulties that may arise, and create the conditions that will ensure the highest probability of success.

To prepare fully, the manager creates a short written summary of the essential information that will be needed in the meeting. This information is simply the data that the manager collected in the previous step. The written summary should include brief statements of the following:

1. *The category the problem falls into: performance, attendance or conduct.* Noting the category at the top of the page will help get the conversation back on track if irrelevant issues lead the discussion astray. This will also help the manager communicate that there is one specific area of performance that he is concerned with.

2. *The dates of any previous conversations about this or similar problems.* Having the actual dates available is invaluable should the employee claim that this is the first time the issue has been raised.

What if the previous conversations were informal and no written record was made of them? The fact that no record was made does not negate the fact that they actually took place. If the employee says that he doesn't recall the conversation, acknowledge the fact that sometimes people do forget things and that's why you went to the trouble of jotting down some notes about the discussion. Then suggest that the subordinate make a note of the fact that the two of you are talking now, because the situation has now become more serious.

What if you can't recall the specific date? Again, just because you can't come up with the precise date that the conversation occurred does not discount the fact that it did in fact happen. Simply estimate the date as accurately as possible: "We talked about this around three weeks ago, Walt, and at that time . . ."

3. *The specific statements of expected performance and actual performance.* This is the most important part of the written summary. Here the manager is writing in simple, clear, and unarguable terms exactly what the performance expectation is and precisely how the employee is failing to meet that expectation.

In the attendance category both the expectation and the actual performance will be quite easy to specify. The desired performance is for the employee to arrive at work on time every day; the actual performance is that in the past four weeks, on May 5, 11, 16, and 22, Sally Edwards reported for work more than twenty minutes late.

Similarly, when the problem is in the conduct area, the difference between actual and desired is usually very clear: The desired performance is that supervisors wait until the Personnel Change Notice form is returned by the compensation department before advising an employee that he has been granted a salary increase; the actual performance is that Marilyn Longer told George Schmidt that he would be getting a raise before the paperwork was processed.

In the performance arena the difference between what we want and what we get may be murky. It may be difficult to pinpoint one specific behavior, or even a collection of specific shortcomings, that creates the need for a formal discussion. In these cases, the manager may have to continually ask himself: "For example . . . ?" as he attempts to move his generalizations and judgments about the individual into accurate and defensible illustrations of performance deficiencies.

4. *A summary of the good business reasons why the problem needs to be solved.* Compiling a list of the effects of the problem helps the employee understand why what he is doing is a problem. It also helps produce the employee's agreement to solve that problem.

To generate a complete list, assume that the individual has said, "I don't really think that what I am doing is a problem. What difference does it make?" How would you respond?

Most managers find it fairly easy to generate a list of a half dozen good business reasons why a problem must be solved, particularly when they consider the impact of the situation on fellow employees, customers (both internal and external), the culture of the organization, the perceptions of others of the individual and the work group as a whole, and the effects on the manager himself.

5. *The list of consequences that are likely to result if the individual chooses not to change and correct the situation.* One consequence that will always appear on the list will be "Further disciplinary action up to and including discharge."

While managers usually view the potential for disciplinary action as a serious consequence for misbehavior, employees frequently discount both the likelihood and severity of the threat. Many employees have heard managers thunder, "I'm gonna write you up!" or "I'll fire you if you ever do that again!" so many times that they consider this just one more manipulative game managers play to enforce order and get more work out of the troops. Constantly threatened with write-ups and sackings, they become deaf to the warning of further disciplinary action.

Unable to see past the threat of "further disciplinary action," managers often overlook responses that may have far more persuasive power with difficult employees. If a person refuses to correct a deficiency once it has been brought to his attention, the likely outcomes of being forbidden salary increases, denied promotional opportunities, subjected to closer supervision, and assigned to less desirable tasks may be far more persuasive in convincing the employee of the need to change.

With these notes prepared, the manager is now prepared to begin the discussion with a high probability that both an improvement in performance and an enhanced relationship will result.

Creating the Setting

Too often the decisions about when the meeting will be held, who will be present, the location of the meeting, where participants will sit, the time allotted to it, and other critical matters are made by default. The more that these issues are resolved consciously, the greater the likelihood of overall success.

Where Should the Meeting Be Held?

While the logical place is in the manager's office, there are alternatives to consider. If privacy is a concern, consider using a conference room. If the matter is not yet serious enough to invoke one of the formal Discipline Without Punishment steps, a session at an isolated table in the cafeteria might be effective. If the matter is a very serious disciplinary transaction, the manager may ask his boss if the meeting can be scheduled in the boss's office with the senior manager present as a witness, to increase the perceived seriousness of the issue.

When Should the Meeting Be Held?

The session should follow the discovery of the problem as closely as possible, but sufficient time must be allowed for the manager to investigate the facts and prepare for the meeting.

Too often, managers begin the discussion with an employee about a problem immediately upon uncovering a serious lapse in acceptable performance. By rushing pell-mell into a discussion, the manager loses effectiveness in two ways. First, since he took no time to prepare, he has not thought through the issues of desired and actual performance, the effects and the logical consequences, and thus will be less capable of avoiding distractions and maintaining a professional approach. Worse, since he took no time to prepare, the employee may believe that this is merely a spur-of-the-moment reaction on the manager's part and not a matter of serious concern.

Another scheduling issue involves getting all the necessary approvals before beginning the discussion. In almost every organization a supervisor must get higher management approval before proceeding with one of the more serious steps of the Discipline

Without Punishment procedure. No organization allows a manager to place an employee on Decision Making Leave or terminate the individual without the review of at least a human resources representative and a member of the senior management team. These things frequently take time, and as the time between the commission of the act and the discussion of the issue expands, the impact of the discussion on the employee may decrease.

Effective implementation of the complete Discipline Without Punishment procedure always simplifies the approval process, but time obstacles created by out-of-town trips, vacations of key approvers, and other schedule dilemmas may still interfere with discussing the matter with all deliberate speed. When time delays occur, it may be wise to say to the employee, "This situation is one that concerns me a great deal, and we will need to talk about it seriously. I will get back to you as soon as I can and set a time for a meeting to discuss it. In the meantime, it is important that you immediately follow all job procedures."

Of course, in some situations the employee's presence on the premises cannot be tolerated during the investigation period. Later, in discussing the procedures for a crisis suspension in Chapter 9, we will explore in detail how to handle these difficult and complex situations.

What Are the Room Arrangements?

Room arrangements rarely make much difference in achieving the goal of gaining the employee's agreement. The most important decision the supervisor needs to make is whether he wishes to increase his perceived power or increase the informal nature of the meeting.

If the problem is essentially minor and the supervisor does not want to come across as overbearing, moving out from behind the desk and sitting at a conference table or some other more egalitarian setting may have the desired effect. On the other hand, it may well be appropriate for the supervisor to deliberately increase his perceived power. In this case, such minor items as putting on his suit coat, sitting behind the desk, maintaining a firm and upright posture, and removing all paper from the desk except for the notes he had made for the conversation communicates a grave atmosphere that may produce serious reflection.

(In a seminar once, a manager admitted that he had secretly placed both a telephone directory and a dictionary on his chair before meeting with a particularly recalcitrant troublemaker. Being able to look down on the individual greatly increased his perceived power in the situation.)

Who Should Participate?

The two principal players are the employee and the immediate supervisor. Everyone else is secondary.

If the employee is represented by a union, the shop steward or other union representative should be present during the discussion. If the discussion is intended to be a formal disciplinary transaction, it should not begin without the presence of the appropriate union representative. Even if the discussion is planned to be a nondisciplinary coaching session, it is often wise to ask the employee if he wants a shop steward to be present and to advise the union representative about the problem and the discussion the manager had about it.

While the presence of a union representative often may appear to make it more difficult to conduct a productive discussion, the representative's presence may reinforce the idea with the employee that this is indeed serious business. Even if the shop steward is combative and confrontive during the meeting, it may well be that after the session has ended, as the employee and the steward are walking back to the workplace, the steward may throw a friendly arm around the employee's shoulder and say, "Look, pal. I put on a show in there for you. But you need to know that if you keep this up there's not much that the union can do for you."

Should other members of management be present? The two who most often attend these discussions are the supervisor's immediate boss and a representative from the personnel or human resources department. Usually, the more people present, the less effective the discussion. The employee may feel overpowered and ganged up on; in this case he is likely to agree to anything just to get out of the situation, with no real intention of following through on any glib commitment to change.

Worse, the opposite situation may happen. The employee may be able to play one person off against another, listening to one person and redirecting questions to someone else, so that nothing of substance gets accomplished.

There may be reasons to have a witness present during the conversation, but his role should be just that: a witness, not a significant participant. The primary reasons for having a witness present are:

- To increase the perceived level of seriousness by the employee. This is particularly beneficial at the later stages of disciplinary action.
- To confirm the supervisor's recollection of exactly what happened during the meeting if required at a later date.
- In cases where the supervisor is unskilled in conducting disciplinary transactions, to allow a "coach" for the supervisor to be present if needed. In this case, the supervisor and the other individual should discuss in advance the conditions under which the "coach" would become an active participant in the transaction.
- In cases where the issue to be discussed is either extremely complicated technically or there are specific legal aspects to the situation, to make sure that the technical or legal aspects are properly addressed.
- In the event that there is any concern with the possibility that the employee may react inappropriately, to reduce the likelihood of a situation involving workplace violence.

How Long Should the Meeting Take?

The time devoted to the meeting will vary depending on the subject to be discussed and the players involved. The most common problem is that meetings like this take too much time, rather than not enough. It is usually more effective to have more short and well-planned meetings than a few long meetings that ramble and meander.

The time of the meeting should be proportionate to the goals to be accomplished. In every meeting the primary goal is to gain the employee's agreement to solve the problem. The manager achieves this by reviewing exactly what the problem is and then asking for the employee's agreement to correct the situation. Even if the manager has to go beyond describing the problem itself and has to discuss the adverse effects and the logical consequences, probably not more than five minutes or so will be necessary.

Once agreement has been gained, more time may be spent on reviewing the possible actions the employee might take to solve the problem. It may be appropriate to engage in some mutual goal setting or for the manager and the employee to develop a joint plan of action. There may be great value in requiring the employee to construct a PIP (Performance Improvement Plan) that they will review in a subsequent meeting. There may be still other issues that arise during the course of the discussion that are worth talking about while the manager and subordinate are together, once the basic agreement has been achieved.

If the transaction is a formal disciplinary discussion, a few minutes will be taken to explain to the employee that this is a formal level of the Discipline Without Punishment procedure. The manager needs to review the organization's procedures and explain how the incident will be documented.

With all this, the total time devoted to the discussion, from the time the employee enters the office until the two of them shake hands and get back to work, rarely needs to extend more than twenty minutes.

With all preliminary procedures and requirements settled, the manager can now begin the actual coaching or disciplinary discussion.

Opening the Discussion

Perhaps the most difficult ten seconds in a manager's life occur at the moment when a subordinate shows up at his door for a scheduled coaching session or disciplinary discussion, sticks his head in and says, "You wanted to see me, Boss?"

The manager knows that if he is able to get the meeting off to a good start the chances of overall success will be great. But if the meeting gets off to a bad start, if the discussion sputters and becomes awkward, he may spend the whole time simply trying to get things back to normal. How do you get things off to a good start?

The conventional advice is correct: Put the employee at ease.

But the conventional suggestion about how to put the individual at ease—talk about matters other than the subject at hand—invariably serves to worsen the situation. Managers are given such wrong-headed advice as, warm up to the subject by talking about how things are going at home, or spend a minute on his hobbies or interests. Having swallowed a dose of this psychological snake oil, the manager starts the conversation off with a chipper discussion of how the local ball team is doing. Worse, the manager may start by asking, "How are things going?" and then, when the employee responds that things are terrific and that no problems of any kind exist, will be in the awkward position of having to disabuse the individual of his notion that all is well.

Stop the palaver. When the manager asks the employee to meet with him for a discussion, the employee knows that the manager has a specific concern, and that concern has little to do with the fortunes of the local ball club or how the garden is coming along. How, then, can the manager put the employee at ease? By getting right to the point.

"Joe," the manager begins, "I've got a problem, and I need your help." With those ten words, the manager has accomplished four worthwhile ends. First, simply by using the employee's name he has begun the discussion on a personal basis. One of the most effective ways of enhancing an individual's self-esteem is the remarkably simple technique of using the employee's name. It is virtually impossible to overdo it.

Second, the manager has indeed gotten right to the point. In hardly a second he has let the employee know that the subject of the meeting is a problem that concerns the manager—not the doings of the ball team, or life at home with the wife and the kids, or things in general around the office.

Third, by using an "I message," the manager has prevented the immediate defensiveness that arises when the discussion begins with a heavy "you" emphasis. At this point it is the manager who has a concern; it is the manager who is raising the issue; it is the manager who feels the need for action. At the end of the meeting, the employee may well have a problem. At the start of the meeting, however, defensiveness can be reduced by using an "I statement" rather than opening with a variation on the accusatory "You're causing some difficulties that I need to talk to you about," "You're doing something that you need to stop," "You've got a problem!"

Finally, in his opening words the manager has enlisted the employee's help. There seems to be magic contained in the phrase "I've got a problem and I need your help." The psychologists may explain it in terms of our need to be fulfilled or self-actualized, our need for achievement or desire to be of service. Whatever the reason, the phrase has the uncommon ability to make people immediately react in a way that puts them at your service.

A Good Opening Statement

To get the meeting off on a good start, open with either those exact words or a close variant:

> "Sally, there's something that's concerning me and I need to talk to you about it."
>
> "Ed, I'm dealing with a situation that's troubling me. I need your help in getting it resolved."
>
> "Chris, there's something that's bothering me and I need to see if I can get your help in getting it taken care of."

The use of the magic phrase "I've got a problem and I need your help" will command the individual's attention. Then immediately move to a full description of the concern you just introduced. Explain the problem in terms of actual and expected behavior:

> "At the start of the year, Lucille, you and I agreed that you would visit every site at least twice during the year. We're now into September and your reports indicate that you've been to less than half the sites, and some of those visits were only for an hour or so."
>
> "Here's the issue, Tony. Right or wrong, the company expects that nobody will put any software on their computer without requisitioning it through central supply and paying for it. Louise told me that she was concerned about your borrowing her disks for the MicroCad program and installing it on your machine."

"You know that the roller cover is put on the machine as a safety guard, Dan. A week ago I pointed out that you were running the machine with the cover raised. Then this morning I saw you running the machine once again without the cover in place."

"Charlie, remember that training program we all went through a month or so ago called Building Team Effectiveness? My goal for putting all of us through that was to get us to start acting more like a team and less like a bunch of individual contributors. I tried to say that during the program and when we did the debriefing afterwards. But I haven't seen you act in the ways we talked about during the session.

"Here's what I mean: In Charlene's review meeting yesterday afternoon you were late getting in and then spent most of the time going through the papers you brought with you. When Jack asked for help in doing the final clearcheck on the turbine outflow, you were the only one who didn't contribute. As I recall, what you said was, 'Hey, pal, my bucket's full. . . .' And then this morning you complained that you would need to change your flight plans if we held the Osbourne final run-through at a time that worked out perfectly for everyone but you. I noticed a couple other things, but those are the main ones that concern me."

In each case, the manager clearly communicates exactly what the desired behavior was and exactly how the employee was failing to meet the expectation.

Some of the situations are easy to identify and to explain to the employee. Lucille either visited all of the sites or she didn't; Dan either was working with the safety guard on or he was not. Both what we want and what we get are clear.

The other situations are not so clear-cut. The manager did not accuse Tony of being a software pirate. Instead he stuck to what he knew for sure: that Louise had expressed a concern about his borrowing her disks and installing the program on his machine.

The last situation is the most difficult: Charlie's failure to act as

a team player. In this case there is not a specific deviation from a
clearly defined standard. Instead, Charlie's boss has noticed a collection of behaviors that, while individually minor and perhaps insignificant, taken together support his contention that Charlie is not
acting as part of a team. He described three very specific incidents
that supported his conclusion that the broader goal of having everyone support each other as a team was not being met.

Note that in none of these statements made to begin the discussion does the manager accuse the employee or hypothesize about
what might be causing the problem. In a straightforward, businesslike way, the manager makes three statements:

"Here's what I want."
"Here's what I get."
"There is a difference."

Letting the Employee Speak

Having opened the discussion with the useful phrase "I have a problem and I need your help," and having stated clearly the specific
desired and actual performance, the manager now turns the conversational ball over to the employee by saying, "Tell me about it."

Too often, managers lose effectiveness in coaching or disciplinary discussions by talking too much. They talk too much because
they are nervous. The situation is difficult and unfamiliar, there is a
lot at stake, they don't know exactly what to say or what the employee's reaction will be, they feel awkward and ill prepared. So the
way they resolve their awkward and uncomfortable feelings is by
talking. But the more they talk, the less effective they become.

Ask any manager for his recommendation about who should
do the most talking in a coaching session and he will instantly tell
you: the employee. But tune in on a typical conversation and you'll
discover that it's the manager who's talking far more than 50 percent
of the time.

The reason that managers talk so much in the opening of the
transaction is that they don't know how to hand off the conversational ball to the employee gracefully. All that it takes, however, is
the phrase "Tell me about it" or some minor variant on the theme.

The model for opening the conversation is simple and direct:

I've got a problem and I need your help. Here's what it is. . . . Tell me about it. And then the manager shuts up and lets the employee speak.

Of course, "Tell me about it" can be replaced by any roughly equivalent transition statement that will work equally well:

"What can you tell me about this?"
"Is there something I should know?"
"Is my understanding accurate?"

In each case, the statement serves to turn the responsibility for the conversation over to the employee without causing defensiveness. The goal is problem solving, not accusation. Asking the employee "What do you have to say for yourself?" will probably not achieve this end.

Each of the above examples of opening transactions involved at most ten to twenty seconds, a far shorter period than most managers spend in getting the discussion under way. But one of the reasons why this approach is so effective is that it is so short: The manager says nothing that will give the employee an opportunity to rebut the manager's statement unless the manager is simply flat dead wrong. And in those unusual cases where the manager has initiated a discussion based on bad data, the effect of using this opening will reduce the awkwardness since there have been no accusations or threats of disciplinary action made.

Having turned the discussion over to the employee, the manager is now obliged to listen to what the employee has to say.

But ask a manager "What are you listening for?" and he will experience great confusion. Instead of telling you exactly what he is listening for, he will explain why listening is a good thing. It communicates an interest in what the employee has to say, he responds. It helps build the relationship; it may provide information on the cause of the problem or the possible solutions that might be employed to correct it.

Listening carefully certainly indicates that you really are interested in what the other person has to say. By listening, you send a message that the other person, his feelings and perceptions, are really important to you. You get a better understanding of someone else and how that person looks at things.

The Key Aim of Listening

But while all of these things are true, there is one specific objective that we have when we listen to the employee in the opening of a coaching or disciplinary discussion: *to confirm that the action we have planned is appropriate.*

At this point in the transaction you have identified the problem in terms of expected and actual behavior. You have determined the effects of the problem and the logical consequences that the employee can expect if he chooses not to correct the situation. Based on that, you have also determined the appropriate action to take.

But up to this point, you haven't talked to the person. And while it doesn't happen very often, it is possible that there may be some additional information that you are unaware of that could cause you to change your mind about what the best course of action should be.

For example, let's say that you notice one morning that one of your employees is not at his desk. Since you have had two previous discussions about his tardiness problem, you decide to conduct a formal Oral Reminder discussion with him as soon as he comes in.

You begin the conversation by saying, "Bill, I have a problem. We've talked twice before about the importance of being at work on time every day, and once again you're late. Is there anything that I need to be aware of?"

But instead of offering the anticipated lame excuse Bill says, "Yeah, there sure is! Yes, I was late getting in, but the reason I was late was that just as I was coming in the shop superintendent saw me and told me that there had been an accident near the tooling shed and to go to the back gate and watch for the ambulance and send it to the shed when they arrived!" In this case, any form of formal disciplinary action would probably be inappropriate. But had the manager opened the discussion by saying, "Bill, I called you in here to give you an Oral Reminder for coming in late this morning," he would find it difficult to proceed once Bill reveals the reason for his tardiness. Assuming that Bill is telling the truth, the manager is now in the awkward position of either having to retract something he has already announced or proceed with something he no longer feels is appropriate.

That's why you have one specific purpose in listening to the employee: to confirm that there is no other information that could cause you to change your decision about the appropriate action to take. For this reason it is best to wait until the end of the conversation to announce to the employee that the discussion is a formal disciplinary transaction, unless by union contract the supervisor is required to tell the employee that the discussion is disciplinary before he can begin.

Gaining the Employee's Agreement

Once you have listened to the employee's response and confirmed that there is no reason not to proceed with the action you have planned, discuss the situation with the objective of gaining the person's agreement to change.

Most of the time you'll be able to get the employee's agreement to solve a problem simply by asking for it. Review your statements of actual and expected performance and then ask the employee to agree to do the job as it should be done:

Manager: Janet, I've got a problem and I need your help.

Employee: A problem?

Manager: Yeah. Remember two weeks ago when Morley called about the Harrison estimate? You said you'd get on it right away but apparently nothing's happened. He called me this morning and he was livid. What's the story?

Employee: Well, to tell you the truth I got behind on it and I didn't get it out. There's been so much going on that a couple of things are bound to fall through the cracks. I'll take care of it right away.

Manager: I know we're busy, but this is now the third time we've had to talk about getting project work done as scheduled. I mentioned it to you last month and then a few weeks ago we talked specifically about deadlines when the Lanaham deadline was missed. I'm concerned about the

Harrison estimate, but my real concern is that you aren't getting your jobs done on time.

Employee: Well, I've just been busy. . . . It's been crazy around here for a while.

Manager: I know that. I also know that the work we accept has to be produced when it's due. I need you to agree that in the future every project you've got will be out on the agreed date.

Employee: Well, I do try, but sometimes things get in the way.

Manager: I know they do. I need you to come and talk to me as soon as you see a problem comes up and the deadline is in trouble. But I do need your agreement that you'll meet those deadlines every time.

Employee: Well I guess I can do that. . . .

Manager: What do you mean?

Employee: I mean that I will meet all of the deadlines from now on.

Manager: That's great, Janet. Can we consider this case closed?

Employee: Sure. Case closed.

Manager: Thanks.

In this case the manager was clear about the gap between actual and desired performance and clearly asked for the employee's agreement to solve the problem: "I need you to agree that in the future every project you've got will be out on the agreed date." When the employee made an initial move in the direction of providing the agreement—"I guess I can do that"—the manager got her to confirm that the agreement was real by asking, "What do you mean?" The result was a clear statement of her agreement to meet the expectation: "I mean that I will meet all of the deadlines from now on."

Another Example

Most people will agree to solve the problems they create once those problems have been brought to their attention in a calm, professional, businesslike way. Occasionally the manager may need to explain the adverse effects caused by the problem in order to provoke the agreement:

Manager: Thanks for coming in, Sal. There's an issue that's concerning me that I need to get your help in resolving.

Employee: Sure, what's the trouble?

Manager: Calls and contacts.

Employee: Calls and contacts? We just talked about that a week or so ago—and now you want to talk about it again?

Manager: That's right, Sal. When we talked last time I went over exactly what expectations we have for you and everybody else in telephone sales. It's sixteen calls an hour, sixteen contacts a day. You're still a long way away. . . . What's the problem?

Employee: Sixteen/sixteen is an awful lot. Besides, I make better contacts than anybody else. Almost every one of the contacts I make ends up to be a buyer. Nobody else gets the quality of contacts that I do. It's quality that's important, not quantity, isn't it?

Manager: Quality is important, Sal, and I've got no problems with the quality of contacts you make.

Employee: Damn right.

Manager: But that's not the issue. I need you to agree that you will meet the basic expectation of making a minimum of sixteen calls an hour, and out of those make direct contact with sixteen qualified prospects every day.

Employee: I can't promise that. I can't control who answers the phones or the kinds of leads I get.

Manager: Do you know why it's important, Sal?

Employee: Because you say so.

Manager: Not because I say so. Because it actually does make a difference. That standard has been in place for almost two years, and it's a reasonable one. If we don't have a target then we don't know how we're doing. If you don't make your calls, other people figure it's not important. They start sliding too.

Employee: Well talk to them, then.

Manager: I do. I talk to everyone who doesn't make the sixteen/sixteen standard. That's why we're talking now, Sal. I know that you can do it. I just need you to agree that you will.

Employee: And if I don't?

Manager: You know the answer to that. We'll talk again, but next time it will be a formal disciplinary transaction. I'll also require that you report your results to me on an hour-by-hour basis.

Employee: Like we were back in fourth grade, huh?

Manager: Sal, come on. I don't want to ask you for hourly reports any more than you want to be forced to provide them. What I do want is for you to agree to solve this problem and get back to doing the job right. Can I have your agreement?

Employee: Yeah, sure.

Manager: Sal, what are you actually agreeing to do?

Employee: I'm agreeing to do what you're telling me I gotta do.

Manager: And what is that?

Employee: To make sixteen calls an hour and generate sixteen good contacts a day.

Manager: Will you do it?

Employee: Yeah, I'll do it.

Manager: Sal, are we ever going to have to talk about this again?

Employee: No. I'll get it done.

Manager: Do we have a deal?

Employee: Sure.

In this case the manager had to discuss both the adverse effects of the problem and the logical consequences if the employee failed to meet the expectations. But focusing on the specific issue allowed the manager to gain the agreement and close the conversation on a productive note.

Whatever the subject to be discussed, and regardless of whether the transaction is a nondisciplinary coaching session, an Oral Reminder, or a Written Reminder, the procedure is the same:

1. Open the conversation by getting directly to the point: I have a problem; here's what it is . . . ; tell me about it.
2. Listen to what the employee has to say to make sure that the action you are planning to take is appropriate.

3. Ask the employee for agreement. If you gain agreement, wrap the discussion up. If you fail to gain agreement, discuss the adverse effects of the problem, and if necessary, the logical consequences the employee will face if he chooses not to correct the situation.
4. End the discussion by communicating a positive expectation of change.

What If the Problem Continues?

The individual has agreed to solve a problem, but the problem arises again. What next?

Obviously, another conversation with the individual is held. This time, two additional steps are taken:

1. The manager reviews the employee's failure to live up to the previous agreement.
2. The manager and the employee explore the specific action the employee will take to ensure a permanent correction of the situation.

In the initial conversation, the manager and the employee may have discussed various things that the individual might do to make sure that the problem is corrected. In many cases the steps that the person must take are obvious. Certainly for problems in the conduct category, the solution is plain: Follow the rule. For an employee with a problem of smoking in a restricted area, no grandiose plan of action is required to eliminate it. He simply must not smoke where it's not permitted.

Problems in the performance and attendance categories may take more planning and action on the employee's part to solve:

Manager: Michael, when we talked last time you agreed that we would never have to talk about your coming to work late again. But the problem continues. What's going on?

Employee: Well, Becky, when we talked before, I didn't know that my wife was going to be switched to the three-to-eleven shift at the hospital. And I certainly didn't know that the transmission and the brakes on my car would both give out at the same time. These things happen. Give me a break.

Manager: These things do happen, Michael, and if you had brought them to my attention I'm sure we could have worked something out. But when you decide not to let me know about what's going on and choose to deal with your problems by coming in to work late, those decisions on your part affect the decisions that I make.

Employee: Wait a minute! I didn't *decide* not to tell you; I just forgot. I didn't *choose* to come to work late. It just happened, that's all.

Manager: Michael, those things really are decisions and choices. You are responsible for arranging your affairs so that you can do what we pay you to do. At a minimum, that means showing up. When you decide not to do that, whether it's a conscious decision or not, I have to deal with the decisions and choices you make.

Employee: I want to be here every day. I really do. I just ran into a shot of bad luck, that's all.

Manager: This is serious, Michael. I need you to agree that you will be here on time every day.

Employee: I'll try. . . .

Manager: I'm glad you'll try, Michael, but what I need is a real commitment.

Employee: OK, I'll be here every day.

Manager: On time?

Employee: On time.

Manager: How will you do that?

Employee: Huh?

Manager: You agreed to be here every day on time in our last conversation, Michael, but you didn't live up to it. What are you going to do differently this time so you can honor that commitment?

Employee: Well, like I said, I'll try harder.

Manager: Come on, Michael. What are you really going to do?

Employee: I'm taking the car into the shop tomorrow, and I can arrange for a ride with Roy in case it's not ready. With Judy's three-to-eleven shift I'll need to leave here right on time to pick up the kids at the day care, but that shouldn't be a problem. And I can make a backup arrangement with Roy in case I run into car problems again.

Manager: Will you do that?

Employee: Yeah.

Manager: Do we have an agreement?

Employee: Yeah, we do.

Revisiting the Agreement

It may happen that in spite of making an original agreement to correct a problem, an individual continues the inappropriate behavior even after a subsequent conversation in which the agreement was reviewed and various alternative solutions that would ensure that the person could live up to his agreement were discussed. In this case, the manager needs to be blunt about the consequences of the person's choice not to honor an agreement that he has made. At this point the problem is no longer merely a continuation of the original incident. The real problem is the employee's failure to live up to his agreement:

Manager: Sal, two weeks ago we talked about calls and contacts. At that time you agreed that you would make sixteen calls an hour and sixteen contacts a day. I just got the weekly summary from last week. You averaged thirteen calls and nine contacts.

Employee: Yeah, but it was a tough week, and some of those calls took a real long time. I'll do better next week.

Manager: Doing better isn't the issue any more, Sal.

Employee: You mean thirteen calls and nine contacts is OK?

Manager: No. It's unacceptable and you know that it's unacceptable. But that's not what we're here to talk about.

Employee: It's not?

Manager: No. What I need to talk to you about is your agreement. You agreed that you would make sixteen calls an hour and sixteen contacts a day, and you decided not to live up to it.

Employee: Yeah, but I meant to.

Manager: Whatever your intentions were, Sal, the fact is still the same: You made an agreement with your boss, and you decided not to honor it.

Employee: Well, gee, I didn't look at it that way.

Manager: Is there something wrong with looking at it that way?

Employee: No, not exactly, but it sounds real serious when you put it like that.

Manager: It is serious, and that is exactly the right way to put it. Tell me something, Sal. If you decide not to live up to the agreements that you make with your customers, what do you think will happen?

Employee: They'll stop doing business with me.

Manager: That's right. And what will happen if you decide not to live up to the agreements you make with your boss?

Employee: You'll fire me?

Manager: Yes, Sal, I will. If you choose not to honor your agreements, what basis do we have for an employment relationship?

Employee: Well, if you put it like that, I guess we don't have any basis.

Manager: That's right. That's why it's important, when you make an agreement, that you live up to it. Now are you able to agree to make the sixteen calls and sixteen contacts?

Employee: I guess I really don't have any choice.

Manager: Not if you want to work here, you don't. You know exactly what the job requires, Sal. The question is, do you still want it?

Employee: Yeah. Of course I want my job.

Manager: Then I need your agreement that you'll do what's required.

Employee: Well, sure. Now that you put it that way, of course I agree.

Manager: That's great, Sal. Now let's talk about what you need to do to make sure that you can actually live up to that agreement. . . .

A Matter of Choice

In the previous two examples, the manager concentrated on talking to the employee in terms of "decisions" and "choices." As the manager in the first example said, "But when you *decide* not to let me know about what's going on and *choose* to deal with your problems by coming in to work late, those decisions on your part affect the decisions that I make." In the second example the manager said, "You agreed that you would make sixteen calls an hour and sixteen contacts a day, and you *decided* not to live up to it."

One of the fundamental principles of Discipline Without Punishment is the recognition that performing well or poorly, coming to work on time or late, following or breaking the rules, and living up to or disregarding one's agreements are matters of choice. The coaching procedure used in all Discipline Without Punishment transactions reinforces this basic idea that people are responsible for their behavior and performance. The concept of personal responsibility for one's own actions is the essence of Discipline Without Punishment.

Locus of Control

Many people who encounter performance problems in organizations and fail to live up to their agreements believe that they have little control over what happens to them and that they are for the most part pawns of fate. The psychological term for this phenomenon is *locus of control*. Locus of control refers to the extent to which individuals believe that they can exert control over the events that affect them. Some people (*internalizers*) see themselves as masters of their own fate, captains of their own souls. They believe that they are autonomous and take personal responsibility for what happens to them, good or bad. They believe that the events of their lives, for the most part, are a function of their actions and decisions. Their locus of control is internal.

Other people (*externalizers*) believe that they ultimately bear little personal responsibility for what happens to them or for their actions and decisions. Those with an external locus of control believe that events in their lives are primarily determined by factors outside their control: by chance, by fate, by other people. Externalizers will argue that making a lot of money is simply a matter of getting the right breaks; internalizers believe that raises are earned by hard work. Externalizers are likely to say that it's just about impossible to figure some people out; internalizers will argue that getting along with people is a skill that must be practiced. Internalizers believe that their choices regarding diet and exercise will have a direct effect on their health; externalizers point to runners who die young and smokers who live to be ninety and say, "You never can tell." Internalizers believe that they can change the world around them; externalizers believe that it is pointless to try.

On tests of locus of control, most managers achieve high internalizer scores. They tend to be more achievement oriented and are comfortable with the idea that we are responsible for the choices we make and for the things that happen to us. A person with a low internalizer score would probably be neither happy nor successful as a manager, since we expect managers to exert influence over the world and the people around them.

With their internalizer view of the world, managers can be frustrated when confronted with an individual with an external locus of control. Not only will the externalizer subordinate be likely to write off any failure to meet expectations as simply a matter of "that's the way the ball bounces," the externalizer will also be less likely to accept praise or compliments on a job well done. "Thanks, but it wasn't really me," he is likely to respond. "I just got lucky this time around. That's how it goes sometimes."

The difficulty with managing the externalizer is the individual's inability or reluctance to connect his own choices of behavior with the consequences that those choices produce. If life truly is a matter of luck, chance, and fate, then it is as misguided to reward people with a perfect attendance record as it is to punish those whose absenteeism is intolerable. *Que sera sera.*

Most managers reject the externalizer's argument that chance plays the dominant role in determining what happens to us. The internalizer manager points out that among the common characteristics of those people who had perfect attendance records were that they maintained a regular exercise program; they maintained their weight and ate a healthy diet; they took good care of their cars and had a backup plan if their cars ever developed problems; they got up in the morning early enough that they could leave for work with a sufficient margin of time that an unforeseen traffic jam didn't make them late, etc.

It is about as difficult to convince a person with an external locus of control to take personal responsibility for his behavior as it would be to explain to a highly successful manager that her success is simply a function of good luck, that her pleasant circumstance is no more a function of her hard work than is the lottery winner's mansion a manifestation of that individual's personal skill at divining what the string of winning numbers would be. Somebody had to win the lottery; somebody had to be named senior vice president—the dynamics are the same.

Building Personal Responsibility

The manager can increase the probability that the employee will change and resolve a problem if the manager discusses the need for change in terms of the choices the employee makes. We each have the capability for choice; the coaching process makes that capability a part of the system.

It is always appropriate for the manager to consider in advance the various approaches or solutions the employee might use in attempting to resolve a problem. But it is important to recognize that the responsibility for finding a solution to the problem is the employee's, not the manager's. If the manager makes a suggestion that the employee accepts and it subsequently turns out that the suggestion was not effective in solving the problem, the employee can turn back to the manager and say, "See! I did what you told me and it didn't work!" So while the manager may assist the employee by making suggestions or offering guidance, the burden of actually solving the problem is always borne by the individual.

Dealing with Discussion Difficulties

Most coaching sessions will proceed without difficulty if the manager prepares effectively for the transaction, focuses the discussion on gaining the employee's agreement to change, and concentrates on the joint objectives of solving the problem and enhancing the relationship. Difficulties, however, are always waiting to challenge even the most experienced manager/coach. Typically these discussion difficulties present themselves as games played by the employee. While the employee may not consciously intend or even be aware that he or she is attempting to engage the manager in a manipulative game, the fact remains that there are communication games the unwary manager can be sucked into.

Unlike real life games, these treacherous communication games are ones that the manager cannot win. The only way to deal with them is to confront them and move on.

The "Yeahbut" Game

The "Yeahbut" game, first described by psychologist Eric Berne in his book *Games People Play*,[1] arises when the manager attempts to be helpful to the subordinate by suggesting possible courses of action for the subordinate to take in order to solve the problem the subordinate faces:

Manager:	Sally, you've got to be here on time every day.
Employee:	Yeahbut with six kids to get up in the morning it sure is tough to get to work on time.
Manager:	Well, Sal, maybe if you got your kids up a little earlier in the morning you could get them off to school earlier and then get to work on time.
Employee:	Yeahbut the kids stay up so late it sure is tough to get them up in the morning.
Manager:	Well, Sal, maybe if you put the kids to bed a little earlier at night you could get them up a little earlier in the morning.
Employee:	Yeahbut you know my husband works the second shift and they sure like to stay up and see their daddy come home.
Manager:	Well, Sal, maybe if . . .
Employee:	Yeahbut . . .

1. Eric Berne, *Games People Play* (New York: Ballantine, 1985).

And it keeps on going. It turns out that for every piece of good advice that the manager has, the employee always has one more "yeahbut." And when the employee has delivered that one last "yeahbut" and the manager is unable to come up with any more good advice, what the employee has done is successfully demonstrate that the problem cannot be solved. Sally sweetly summarizes, "If you—my boss, my leader, my source of truth and wisdom and light—can't figure out how to solve this problem, how could you ever expect poor little me to?"

Whenever you hear the word *yeahbut*, recognize that you are being sucked into a game. It is a game that you cannot win. The only escape is agreement. Agree with whatever objection the employee has raised and turn the responsibility back where it belongs:

> *Manager:* You're right, Sally. That is a real problem. I agree. It would be difficult for me, too. How are you planning to handle that situation so that you can meet your responsibility of being here every day?

And when Sally responds, "Gee, I don't know," an appropriate response from the manager could be, "Well Sally, you need to think about that carefully, because I need someone in this job who can be here every day, and I sure hope that person is you."

The "Silence" Game

The "Silence" game is invoked when the employee chooses not to respond to the manager's attempts to discuss the problem. In some cases, the silence is understandable because, out of apprehension or anxiety, the individual simply becomes so tongue-tied that he cannot speak. The more sinister form of the silence game arises when the employee uses silence as a vehicle for intimidation.

Silence can be used to intimidate. The important question is, Who's going to be intimidated?

There is no reason for the manager to be intimidated by the employee's silence. If the cause of the silence appears to be the employee's anxiety, a pause and a gentle question like, "Are you feeling OK?" will usually be enough to get the person to respond so that the discussion can continue. But when silence is deliberate and the employee obstinately refuses to respond, a different tack is called for.

"Refusing to engage in a business discussion," or "engaging in inappropriate behavior during a business meeting" are disciplinary offenses that the individual may be confronted with if he obstinately refuses to discuss a problem. In fact, they are a form of insubordination in which the employee is willfully failing to perform a normal part of his job: discussing his performance with his boss.

After one or two questions have gone unanswered and the manager is suspicious that he is encountering an insubordination situation, the following dialogue might well be appropriate:

Manager: . . . So that's my concern, Bill. I need you to agree that in the future you won't clock out until your shift is officially over.

Employee: [*Silence*]

Manager: Is there a problem, Bill? I need your agreement that you will follow this procedure.

Employee: [*Silence*]

Manager: Bill, if you are refusing to discuss this situation it is a very serious matter. Are you refusing to respond to my request?

Employee: [*Silence*]

Manager: Bill, I am now giving you a direct order to discuss this situation with me and get it resolved. If you refuse to obey my order, you will be committing an act of insubordination. This is a very serious offense. You will be subject to discharge if you continue to refuse. Are you willing to discuss this situation?

Employee: [*Silence*]

Manager: Bill, this meeting is over. We will get together later to discuss what has become a very serious matter of insubordination.

At this point the employee should return to the workplace, or perhaps more wisely, be suspended pending investigation and advised to leave the workplace immediately. Most organizations would recommend that the security function be called and for the employee to be escorted from the factory or office.

This scenario, proceeding from the employee's original silence through all of his refusals to speak, is rare. Most organizations would consider a Decision Making Leave, the final step of the Discipline Without Punishment system, to be the appropriate response (if they charitably decided not to terminate). Most of the time however, upon being asked if he is specifically *refusing* to speak, an employee will quickly realize that the situation is far more serious than he anticipated and will rapidly explain that he is not refusing. At this point an excellent opportunity presents itself to the manager to engage in a bit of coaching about appropriate organizational behavior at a time when the employee is totally ready to absorb it.

The "I'll Try" Game

The manager asks the subordinate to agree to change and do the job properly. "OK, boss," the subordinate cheerfully responds, "I'll try."

Have you gained an agreement?

Of course you have! The subordinate has agreed to try. And the next time you see her filing her nails and reading a magazine when she should be on the phone with customers, what will her response be? "I tried."

Trying doesn't count. Only doing what you're paid to do counts. But when the employee responds with either a gay or a grudging "I'll try," realize that you are actually getting close to a legitimate agreement. Parry the "I'll try," response with acceptance ("That's great, Bertha!") and move toward an actual statement of what the employee will do to make the good intention a reality ("I'm glad to hear that, and I'm sure that you will try. But what will you actually do to make sure that you'll be successful?")

The "Irrelevancy" Game

Sooner or later, every manager, no matter how skilled, will get caught in the irrelevancy trap. Here you are, sailing smoothly along in what most managers would find a very difficult conversation, talking comfortably with the employee about how he will redirect his efforts to ensure ideally acceptable job performance, and then wham! You discover you're in the middle of a discussion of an issue that is absolutely irrelevant to the subject at hand. Here's what usually happens:

> *Manager:*   Wait a minute. That's irrelevant.
> *Employee:* No, it's not.
> *Manager:*   Yes, it is.
> *Employee:* No, it's not!
> *Manager:*   Yes, it is!
> *Employee:* NO, IT'S NOT!

And on and on.

Labeling an irrelevancy as such is unproductive. It only generates arguments. Don't waste your time.

When you realize that you are in the middle of an active discussion concerning an irrelevant topic, the technique to use is, "Dismiss and Redirect." Wait until your counterpart pauses for breath and then say, "As far as the way they used to handle this situation in your old company is concerned, I'd like to talk about that separately. First, I need you to agree to come to work every day."

The key words are *separately* and *first*. The magic "Dismiss and Redirect" technique can be used anytime a conversational counterpart raises an issue that you want to make go away. You don't say that it's irrelevant or unimportant or unconnected with the matter at hand. Instead, you graciously acknowledge its importance and then, with a sweep of misdirection, consign it to the netherworld of irrelevancies and return to the primary issue on your agenda:

> "I appreciate your bringing to my attention the fact that the attendance record of other people in the department should be examined, Betty. I'd like to deal with that separately. First, I need your agreement that you will maintain a fully acceptable record."
>
> "It may well be that no one has ever said anything to you before about taking supplies home, Frank, but I'd like to talk about that separately. First I need you to empty your pockets. . . ."

Note that the term is *separately* and not *later*. *Separately* may well mean "never."

If the employee is raising an issue that could turn out to be important to explore, using the Dismiss and Redirect technique still allows you to accomplish the primary objective of gaining the employee's agreement. Once you have gained the agreement, it is appropriate to bring the earlier redirected issue up for current consideration: "Now that we've resolved this problem of shortages, Matthew, I'd like to go back to what you were saying earlier about there being a lot of places where the company's money was flowing away. What did you have in mind when you said that?"

Closing the Discussion

If the conversation has been a nondisciplinary coaching session, simply thank the person for agreeing to correct the situation and express your confidence that the two of you will never need to talk about the matter again. However, if the discussion is a formal disciplinary transaction, the manager must take two additional steps:

1. Advise the employee that it is a formal disciplinary transaction.
2. Advise the employee which Discipline Without Punishment step is being taken.

The manager should also make sure that the employee understands just what it means to be on a formal level of disciplinary action. He or she should review the company's policies regarding disciplinary action with the person and explain any procedural guidelines. The conversation might sound like this:

Manager: I'm glad you've agreed to solve this problem, Cathy, and I'm sure we won't ever need to talk about it again. Since this is the third time you and I have had to talk about this matter, this conversation is a formal Oral Reminder. It's the first step of the company's discipline procedure. Do you know what that means?

Employee: Well, not really. It's not good, is it?

Manager: It's not good, but it doesn't automatically become part of your personnel record. It is the first formal level of our

Discipline Without Punishment procedure. I will be documenting what we have talked about today, along with your agreement to change, but I'll be keeping those records here in the department. Nothing will go into your permanent file unless we have to talk again. But I don't think we'll need to talk about this again, will we, Cathy?

Employee: No, Mr. Navarro. I'm sure we won't.

Manager: Me too, Cathy. It will officially remain active for six months, which means that if another problem comes up we will consider this incident in deciding what to do about the next one. If there are no further problems, in six months it will be dead and will be taken out of the file. If you'll make a note to talk to me six months from today, I'll pull it out of the file, give it to you, and you can throw it away. Is that fair?

Employee: Sure. Is that all?

Manager: That's it, Cathy. Let's get back to work.

Whether the discussion is a coaching session or a formal disciplinary transaction, the manager's final comments should be directed toward building a positive expectation of improvement.

When the manager has gained the employee's agreement, discussed and decided upon the action the individual will take to solve the problem, advised the employee whether or not the discussion is a formal disciplinary transaction, and expressed a belief that this will be the last time they will ever have to address the matter, the discussion step has been completed.

Part Three

Discipline Without Punishment

Formal Disciplinary Action
(Discipline Without Punishment)

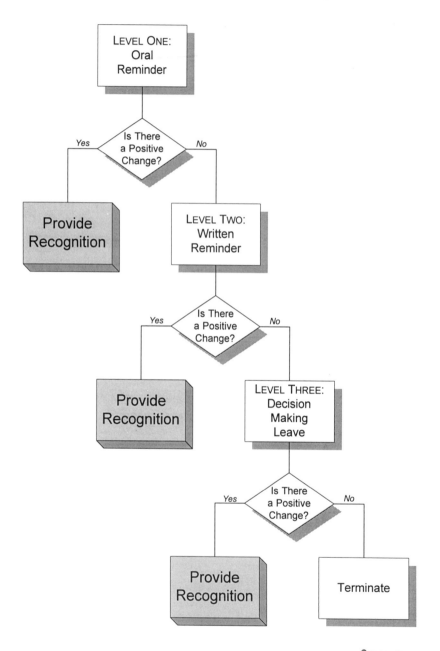

6

The Mechanics of Discipline Without Punishment

Chapter 5 stressed the similarities between a serious but nondisciplinary coaching conversation and the discussion that is held as part of the formal Oral Reminder or Written Reminder steps of the Discipline Without Punishment procedure. This chapter will explore in detail the specific procedures and mechanics for each of these transactions. (The Decision Making Leave is a unique step that will be discussed separately in Chapter 7).

The primary similarities and differences between coaching sessions and initial disciplinary transactions (Oral and Written Reminders) are shown in Figure 6-1.

In reviewing the procedures for each of these steps, I am assuming that the problem being dealt with is one that it is appropriate to start with a coaching session and then move in a step-by-step way through the discipline system if it is not corrected. While this is true of the great majority of problems that managers in organizations encounter, there are those serious issues that are too threatening or potentially damaging to justify starting with a coaching session or even an Oral Reminder. For these situations the appropriate response to a first offense would be a Written Reminder or even a Decision Making Leave.

There are also those offenses which are so grave that the employee has not earned the right to rehabilitation through the organization's disciplinary procedures. For these offenses, like theft or assaulting a customer or co-worker, termination is the most appro-

Figure 6-1. Coaching Sessions and Oral and Written Reminders compared.

SIMILARITIES

	Coaching Session	*Oral/Written Reminder*
Formal element of DWP system?	Yes	Yes
Purpose of discussion?	Gain agreement to correct problem	Gain agreement to correct problem
Planned in advance?	Yes	Yes
Initiator	Immediate Supervisor	Immediate Supervisor
Conducted in private?	Yes	Yes

DIFFERENCES

	Coaching Session	*Oral/Written Reminder*
Formal level of disciplinary action?	No	Yes
Investigation required before action taken?	No	Yes
Documentation required?	Optional (recommended)	Yes
Witness required?	No	Occasionally— policies vary
Limitation on number employee may receive?	No	Yes
Advance approval required?	No	Usually

priate response even when no previous disciplinary action has ever been taken.

In Chapter 8 I review the offenses that are usually considered sufficiently serious to justify skipping the early steps and beginning with a Written Reminder or a Decision Making Leave. I will also review the offenses that usually warrant termination for a first offense, and how that termination should be handled.

Procedures—The Coaching Session

The following subsections discuss how to plan for a coaching session, how to conduct the meeting, and what to do immediately after the meeting.

Before the Meeting

If this is the first time that you and the employee have had to have a formal discussion about a problem (either because it has just come up or because earlier casual conversations have not been effective), make notes for your use during the meeting. The information in these meeting notes will include the category of problem (attendance, performance, or conduct), a specific statement of desired and actual performance, a brief summary of the adverse effects, and the consequences the employee will face if he chooses not to change.

Allow sufficient time for the meeting. Five to ten minutes is usually sufficient to discuss most problems that arise at work, particularly since the conversation is not yet a formal disciplinary transaction. More than twenty minutes is excessive.

Plan where you will hold the conversation. Your office is the logical place; other locations may also be appropriate. Plan where you and the employee will sit.

Arrange for privacy and freedom from interruptions. Since this discussion is not a formal disciplinary transaction, a ringing telephone or a brief interruption won't be lethal. As the transaction moves to a more serious level, it becomes more important that all distractions be avoided.

During the Meeting

As soon as the employee comes into the room or office, begin the meeting by immediately getting to the issue at hand. Use the model described in the previous chapter (begin the conversation by saying, "I have a problem and I need your help"; review the actual and desired performance; invite the employee to respond by asking, "What can you tell me?" or some similar statement.)

In listening to what the individual says, be sensitive to any indicators that the problem may result from either a deficiency in knowledge (where additional training or skill building may be more appropriate) or a deficiency in execution (where job engineering efforts may be required). Listen also to determine whether the cause of the problem might be a situation best addressed through your Employee Assistance Program or by a referral to a church, community service, or United Way agency.

Tell the individual the specific change you are seeking and gain his agreement to solve the problem. The most useful and straightforward way to gain someone's agreement, of course, is simply to ask for it: "Bill, I need you to agree that you will always respond to customer inquiries within two days." Or, "Elizabeth, it is important that no customer be kept waiting unnecessarily. May I have your agreement that whenever you are doing paperwork and a customer comes up you will pause in your paperwork and attend to the customer's needs?"

Once the employee has agreed to perform properly in the future, feel free to discuss any significant issues that the individual may have raised earlier. Discuss the specific action that the employee will take to solve the problem and, if appropriate, the action that you as the manager will take to assist in the effort.

Close the meeting by creating a "self-fulfilling prophecy" that this will be the last time that the two of you will ever need to discuss the matter. If necessary, explain that the discussion has been a coaching session and not a formal disciplinary transaction. Shake hands and get back to work.

After the Meeting

While the discussion is still fresh in your mind, summarize it on the same paper that you used for your premeeting notes. Record the date of the session, the employee's exact agreement, and any statements the employee made that may be useful later on. If the employee agreed to take certain actions, make a note of the specific commitment he made. If you agreed to do anything, record that too. File these notes wherever you keep other department personnel information.

After the meeting, follow up on the conversation to make sure that the problem has been solved. After an appropriate amount of time has passed without another instance of the problem, recognize the employee through a discussion on the subject or with an informal note that you have recognized and appreciate the correction.

Procedures—Oral Reminder

The following subsections discuss how to plan for an Oral Reminder session, how to conduct the meeting, and what to do immediately after the meeting.

Before the Meeting

The procedures for the Oral Reminder are almost identical to those for the coaching session (and will be virtually the same as those for the Written Reminder).

Since this is now a formal disciplinary transaction, it is necessary to conduct a full investigation before beginning the disciplinary transaction. Years ago arbitrator Carroll Daugherty, in rendering his decision in a termination case, promulgated what has become a classic set of questions to determine "whether employer had just and proper cause for disciplining an employee."[1] As Daugherty explained it, "a 'no' answer to any one or more of the following questions normally signifies that just and proper cause did not exist." The questions Daugherty put forth are these:

1. Did the employee clearly understand the rule or policy that was violated?

1. Carroll R. Daugherty, *Grief Bros. Cooperage Corp., supra,* note 7, at 557–559, quoted in James R. Redeker, *Discipline: Policies and Procedures* (Washington, D.C.: Bureau of National Affairs, 1983), pp. 15–18.

2. Did the employee know in advance that such conduct would be subject to disciplinary action?
3. Was the rule that was violated reasonably related to the safe, efficient, and orderly operation of the organization?
4. Is there substantial evidence that the employee actually did violate the rule?
5. Is the disciplinary action planned reasonably related to:
   - The seriousness of the offense?
   - The employee's record with the organization?
   - Disciplinary action taken with other employees who have committed similar offenses?

Review these five questions to make sure that you have "just cause" to proceed. If any question produces a "no" answer, you are not prepared to conduct a disciplinary transaction.

The same notes that you prepared for the coaching session are appropriate for the Oral or Written Reminder transactions: category of problem, desired and actual performance, adverse effects, logical consequences. One additional area may also be appropriate now: If you had an earlier conversation with the employee about the issue and were successful in gaining the individual's agreement to solve the problem, you will want to raise the employee's failure to live up to the agreement for discussion in this meeting. Be sure to note the exact agreement that was made previously.

Many organizations require the supervisor to get approval from his immediate supervisor or department head before conducting the Oral Reminder discussion. Some require human resources to be either advised or to approve in advance before the Oral Reminder discussion takes place. Be sure to review the situation with the appropriate individuals before beginning the conversation.

Should a witness be present? Some organizations require it; others leave it to the supervisor's discretion. A witness to the transaction is particularly appropriate if any of the following conditions are present:

- There is any concern—even remote—that the disciplinary discussion may trigger the possibility of a violent reaction.
- Previous experience with this individual indicates that he is

likely to deny that an agreement was made or even that the conversation took place.

- There is reason to believe that the presence of more than one management representative may appropriately display the importance the organization places on getting the problem resolved.
- There is reason to believe that a false charge of sexual harassment or other type of discrimination charge could be made in retaliation for a disciplinary step being taken.

If the employee is represented by a union, the shop steward or another union representative should be asked to attend, and the meeting should not begin without that person's presence.

Ask the individual and the representative to come into your office. If your boss or another management witness is present, make introductions so that everyone knows who is present and what their purpose in attending the meeting is.

During the Meeting

As with any meeting on an important business issue, get right to the point. This is particularly important if there are several people present besides just the supervisor and the employee. There is no reason to vary from the approach used for the coaching session, opening with "I've got a problem and I need your help in getting it solved," reviewing the desired and actual performance or the rule violation, and then asking the individual to respond.

The balance of the meeting follows the procedures for the coaching session:

- Listen to what the employee has to say to make sure that there is no reason not to proceed with the formal Oral Reminder.
- Review the previous discussions (both casual conversations and any more serious coaching sessions) that you and the employee have had about the situation.
- If a previous discussion resulted in the employee's agreement to correct the situation, indicate that you are concerned not only with the continuation of the original problem but also

with the employee's failure to live up to the agreement that he made.

- Advise the individual of the specific performance change that is required and confirm that he knows exactly what is expected.
- Gain the employee's agreement to solve the problem.
- Advise the employee that this conversation is a formal Oral Reminder.
- Bring the meeting to a close by communicating a positive expectation of change.

One common problem at the Oral Reminder level is the supervisor's failure to state directly that the discussion is a formal disciplinary transaction. Here's how this problem arises. The supervisor and the employee at this point have discussed a business problem in a businesslike way and have reached agreement about its solution. Eager to maintain the good relationship, the supervisor, consciously or inadvertently, may decide not to spoil things by announcing that the discussion has moved beyond a coaching session and is now a formal disciplinary transaction. Believing that the discussion has had the intended effect, that the employee will indeed correct the situation and they will never again need to discuss the issue, he elects not to announce that the discussion is part of the organization's formal discipline procedure.

Sometimes he will be correct. When he is, he will have made a wise decision in veering away at the last minute from calling the discussion a formal discipline step.

Too often, however, the plan goes awry. The employee fails to deliver on his promise and the two of them meet again. Now the supervisor is angry. The problem has continued and the employee has failed to live up to his commitment to change. Worse, he feels taken advantage of. Having given the employee a break, he has been deceived and dealt with in bad faith.

He wants to move to the Written Reminder or directly to the Decision Making Leave. Unfortunately, he has no justification for either, since the Oral Reminder transaction has never taken place.

Because he did not advise the employee that the earlier conversation was an Oral Reminder, it was not. It was just another failed coaching session, and there is no justification for moving from a coaching session to the second step of the discipline system without using the first step first.

"But I did give him an Oral Reminder," the supervisor protests. "I followed all the procedures for the Oral Reminder step. The only thing I didn't do was say the literal words 'This is an Oral Reminder.'"

And because he did not say the literal words "This is an Oral Reminder," therefore it was not. It is the saying of those words that causes a discussion with an employee to be a disciplinary transaction.

One of the more difficult questions for most supervisors to answer precisely is, What makes a disciplinary transaction "disciplinary"? If the supervisor is angry and yells at the employee, is the discussion therefore a disciplinary discussion? If the supervisor discusses the future negative consequences of continued failure to solve the problem, does that make it disciplinary? What if the supervisor threatens to fire the employee if he ever does it again—is that then a disciplinary conversation?

In each case the answer is no. The conversation is not a disciplinary transaction unless and until the supervisor actually tells the employee that is it a disciplinary discussion and advises the individual which one of the three levels of the Discipline Without Punishment system it is.

Consider a parallel phenomenon that arises when people marry. When the bride and groom walk into the church and meet in front of the minister, they are single people. When they walk out of the church, they are married. At some point during the ceremony, they stop being single people and become a married couple. What is the point at which this happens? Is it when they state their vows? Do they change from being single to married when he slips the ring on her finger?

It is not an idle question. Should anything interrupt the ceremony it is critical from a legal standpoint to know whether the participants were married or were still single when the interruption occurred. If a groom dies in the middle of the ceremony, is the woman next to him his fiancée or his widow?

The answer is direct and explicit: the couple end their single lives and become a married couple the instant that the minister says, "And now, by the power vested in me by [the State of Nebraska, or whatever], I pronounce you husband and wife." If the groom dies before the judge says those words, he leaves a fiancée. If he dies after those words are spoken, he leaves a widow.

The same situation prevails in the matter of disciplinary action. Just as the couple are not married until the minister pronounces them so, the conversation between the employee and the supervisor is nothing until the supervisor announces what it is. If it is to be a coaching session, he should say so. And if it is intended to be an Oral Reminder, or any other step of the company's discipline system, he must say so.

Remember the argument among the three baseball umpires. The first one says, "I calls 'em as I sees 'em."

Responds the second, "I calls 'em what they are."

The third counters, "Boys, they ain't nothin' till I calls 'em!"

What is the conversation? It ain't nothin' till the supervisor calls it.

After the Meeting

The key difference in postmeeting activity between the Oral Reminder and the coaching session involves documentation. While it is highly desirable for a record to be made of all coaching conversations, it is not required that they be formally documented. An Oral Reminder, or any formal disciplinary discussion, must be documented.

What is appropriate documentation for an Oral Reminder? And is it not a contradiction for an *Oral* Reminder to be documented?

While it may seem contradictory to say that an Oral Reminder is documented in writing, it is easier to understand and to explain to an employee if we consider what the writing consists of and where the documentation is kept. Most organizations that I have helped to implement Discipline Without Punishment have created a simple form for supervisors to use to make notes in advance of their coaching and disciplinary conversations. This form provides space for the manager to record all of the important information we have already reviewed and to indicate whether the conversation will be a nondisciplinary coaching session or a formal disciplinary transaction.

The form serves as a guideline for the conversation during the meeting. It is an agenda that helps keep the discussion on track and ensures that all critical information will be discussed. After the meeting the supervisor summarizes the details of the discussion, including the employee's agreement to change and any actions the employee agreed to take. If the supervisor also made commitments to help, those should also be recorded. If the employee presented any other significant information, this worksheet is the appropriate place for it to be recorded.

This form, once completed, is all the documentation required for the Oral Reminder. It provides a specific description of the problem itself together with a summary of previous discussions. It includes the employee's agreement to solve the problem and a list of any actions he will take to put the situation behind him. No other writing need be done.

Most companies keep this form within the department and do not forward any copy to the central personnel records. Retaining the Oral Reminder documentation within the walls of the department provides several benefits. Most performance problems that get to the Oral Reminder stage are solved at that stage, so there is no reason for personnel to become involved unless the problem continues and the disciplinary response escalates. In that case, a copy of the Oral Reminder worksheet will simply be attached to personnel's copy of the Written Reminder memo to provide a complete record. Also, by keeping the Oral Reminder documentation within the department, the supervisor can advise the employee that nothing will go into the individual's permanent personnel record unless they have to move to the next step of the system. This can serve as a powerful incentive to change. Lawyers often advise, however, that in the event of litigation a plaintiff may gain access to departmental files. If these files are sloppily kept, there obviously could be adverse consequences. Providing a copy to central human resources may induce better record keeping within departments.

Procedures—Written Reminder

The following subsections discuss how to plan for a Written Reminder session, how to conduct the meeting, and what to do immediately after the meeting.

Before the Meeting

As before, the supervisor conducts an investigation and completes the worksheet listing the critical information required both for discussion during the meeting and the subsequent documentation. Since the worksheet from the previous Oral Reminder will probably be available, most of the information will be readily available.

Virtually every organization requires that before initiating the Written Reminder discussion, the supervisor get approval from one higher level of management in his own department as well as the concurrence of the human resources function.

Some supervisors resent this approval requirement. They feel that since they are the only ones with full information about the situation they are fully qualified to determine what the most appropriate course of action is. Managers frequently complain of squeamish personnel officers who prefer that these untidy situations be handled by less drastic measures.

The purpose of requiring approvals, however, is less to get the "permission" of personnel and senior management than it is to ensure that similar problems are being dealt with in a reasonably parallel manner throughout the organization. While there are some spineless personnel officers who frustrate line managers' attempts to confront problems directly, there are many others who are frustrated by line management reluctance to face up to the need to set high standards and hold people's feet to the fire when they fail to perform.

Necessary approvals obtained, the meeting may begin.

During the Meeting

The manner and approach of the supervisor is unchanged from earlier, less serious transactions. He is serious, calm, dignified, businesslike and unruffled regardless of what the employee's behavior may be. He is a man with a mission who will be undeterred from reaching his objective: to review the existence of a problem with the individual who is creating that problem; to explain why it is a problem and what the logical consequences of failure to correct it will be; and then to secure the employee's agreement that he will, at long last, correct the situation and return to a fully acceptable level of performance. The only indicator that this session is more serious than earlier conversations is the supervisor's reference to previous discussions and the employee's failure to do what he said he would do.

Since previous discussions have not produced the required results, the supervisor now may spend more time discussing the specific things the employee will actually do to solve the problem once and for all. Previously the supervisor may simply have accepted the employee's stated agreement as sufficient; now he will probe behind the words. When the employee proposes an action that might correct the situation, the manager will press the employee, firmly but respectfully, to make good on his intentions:

Manager:	. . . So what will you actually do to get here on time every day, Bob, other than just try harder?
Employee:	Well, like I said, the big problem is my car. The only reason that I'm ever late is that sometimes it doesn't start, or it gives out on the way.
Manager:	So what are you going to do about that?
Employee:	It's basically OK. Mostly it just needs a tune-up and new tires.
Manager:	So what are you going to do?
Employee:	Well, I guess I'll get a tune-up and new tires.
Manager:	That makes sense. When do you plan to do that?
Employee:	Well, gee, I don't know. I don't have a lot of time and money's kind of tight right now.
Manager:	I understand. What do you think you'll do?
Employee:	Well, I could go ahead and get the tune-up done. I could get some of the parts myself and my brother and I could do most of the work this weekend.
Manager:	That seems like a good idea. Will you actually do it?
Employee:	Yeah. I have to do it. I have to get my car back running right.
Manager:	Good. What will you do about the tires?
Employee:	I don't know. I can't afford to get new tires. They're real expensive and I'm tight right now. What do you think I should do?
Manager:	I don't know, Bob. What I do know is that if you can't

	come to work every day on time, you can't work here. We need somebody who can be here every day.
Employee:	Yeah, I guess you're right. But I can't help it if I get a flat.
Manager:	Well, let's be clear about that, Bob. It is your responsibility to be here on time every day. And when you're not here, it really doesn't make any difference whether it's a flat tire or anything else. [*Pause.*] What are you going to do?
Employee:	I'm going to get new tires.
Manager:	How will you do that?
Employee:	Well, I'll see if I can get retreads, and if I can't, I know I can borrow some of the money I need from my sister.
Manager:	Will that solve the problem?
Employee:	Yeah. I won't be late again.

While we won't know until later whether Bob will in fact get his car tuned up and put new tires on it (and, more important, whether he will then start arriving at work on time every day), the supervisor has successfully moved him away from just stating good intentions and into making specific plans. Depending on the situation and the individual, even more planning and problem solving and goal setting might be appropriate.

Throughout the transaction, whether at the Written Reminder level or any earlier one, the supervisor needs to be clear not only about the expected standard of performance but also the employee's responsibility to so arrange the circumstances of his life that he can meet that standard. In the dialogue above, the supervisor did not take the responsibility away from Bob by offering up suggestions for him to reject. Instead he agreed with Bob that Bob was facing a problem. But when asked for advice he appropriately said, "I don't know. What I do know is that if you can't come to work every day on time, you can't work here. We need somebody who can be here every day."

When the supervisor has gained the employee's agreement and discussed exactly what action the individual will take to ensure a permanent correction of the situation, the supervisor must advise the employee that the discussion is a Written Reminder—the second level of the Discipline Without Punishment procedure. Again, it's nothin' till the supervisor calls it.

After the Meeting

The greatest difference between the Oral Reminder and the Written Reminder is the documentation of the two steps. The Oral Reminder is documented by the supervisor's simply completing a discussion worksheet and placing it the department file. To document the Written Reminder the supervisor also completes the discussion form, but the primary documentation of the transaction is a memo confirming the discussion and the employee's commitment to correct the problem.

Documenting disciplinary action is difficult. Early in my career I spent several years working for General Electric. I was one of a handful of recent college graduates selected by GE for their Employee Relations Training Program, a three-year program that involved a half dozen job assignments in various personnel, manufacturing and industrial engineering positions. In one of those assignments I spent most of a year as a first-line supervisor on the second shift in a large electronics plant. Thirty-four female complex assemblers made up my crew.

From time to time, problems arose and disciplinary action was needed. The first time it happened I asked one of my fellow supervisors, an old-timer, what I should do. I was nervous about sitting down and telling this woman, older and far more experienced than I, that her performance was not acceptable.

"Just write her up, call her in, lay it on her, and get back to work," he said. How simple.

I filled out the warning notice form that GE had used for decades. When I had prepared the written document, I planned and practiced what I was going to say. Finally, I asked Carmen to come into the little cubicle I shared with the other supervisors. When she came in I smiled and asked her to sit down, convinced that I was going to be successful in talking with her about the problem, exploring what was causing her to be less than effective, and then engaging in some of the mutual goal setting I had learned about in the classes I had been attending as part of the program. I needn't have bothered.

As soon as I handed her the form and began vocalizing the script I had rehearsed to get our discussion off to a good start, she glanced at it briefly, looked up at me, said, "Screw you, kid!" and walked out.

What went wrong? It wasn't anything I had said, since I hadn't said anything. The problem was the form itself.

The use of a preprinted warning-notice form is one of the most serious deficiencies of the traditional approach to solving discipline problems. When the employee receives the form, he typically reacts to the form itself and not to whatever the supervisor may have written. As soon as the form has been given to the employee, the transaction is complete. The individual has been tried, convicted, and sentenced. Here, take it—don't do it again. Nothing else need be said.

Nothing else need be said as long as our only goal is to build a case strong enough to uphold a termination if subsequently challenged. And back when the obsolete progressive-discipline system was concocted, that probably was sufficient.

Few organizations today see upholding termination as the exclusive purpose of the discipline system. Few, however, have changed their procedures to reflect their change in beliefs. One obvious change is to abolish the antiquated preprinted turkey ticket and replace it with a memo to the employee.

The differences are important. The warning notice form is usually completed before the meeting. This reduces the chance that meaningful discussion will take place once the employee discovers that the form has already been filled out.

Here's a more serious problem. Effective disciplinary documentation provides complete information about the problem itself, the history of the problem, and, most important, the discussion that occurred between the employee and the manager about the problem. If the manager writes the notice before talking to the employee, it is impossible to record any aspects of the discussion. The manager may later come back and add to the notice some comments about whatever the employee said, but for the most part, once the manager has "written him up," whatever has been written remains unchanged.

The Written Reminder Memo

Unlike the preprinted warning notice form, the memo to the employee is written by the supervisor after the meeting has been completed. At the end of the meeting, the supervisor advises the employee that their discussion is a Written Reminder, the second step of the Discipline Without Punishment system, and that he will be writing a memo to the employee confirming their discussion.

When the employee has left, the supervisor completes the discussion form just as he did following the Oral Reminder transaction. He then writes the memo to—not about—the employee.

The following information should be in the memo:

- The names of the supervisor, the employee, and any witnesses who were present
- The date on which the discussion took place (and the location, if significant)
- The specific problem that caused the transaction to occur
- A record of all previous conversations about the problem and the dates on which each of those conversations occurred. This should include formal disciplinary conversations, coaching sessions, and casual conversations (even though no record of the conversation was made). If the individual received an earlier Oral Reminder for this problem, or if the person received this Written Reminder because he was on an active Oral Reminder for an unrelated problem, this fact should be directly stated.
- A statement, in all detail required, of what continuing problems have been experienced since the earlier conversations took place
- A statement that the situation must be corrected (not "improved")
- A statement of the specific change that must be made
- A statement of the fact that failure to correct the problem may lead to more serious disciplinary action
- A statement that in addition to solving the immediate problem, the organization expects the employee to maintain an acceptable level of performance in every area of his job
- A record of the agreement made by the employee to correct the problem
- A record of any action the employee agreed to take in order to bring about the correction
- A closing statement that expresses the supervisor's belief that

the problem will in fact be corrected and that the employee will perform properly in the future

There is a great deal of information to be communicated. Using the above checklist to prepare the documentation memo will make writing the memo easier, ensure that it incorporates all required information, and prevents inappropriate information from slipping in. Figure 6-2 is an example of a Written Reminder memo.

Reviewing the Memo With the Employee

In the traditional approach to discipline, the supervisor writes the warning notice to the employee in advance of the discussion, issues the warning to the employee during the meeting, and files the copies after the meeting. In the Discipline Without Punishment procedure, the disciplinary transaction is documented by writing a memo to the employee summarizing the conversation. Since this memo is written after the meeting has been completed, the manager needs to meet with the employee again to review the Written Reminder memo.

Many managers are initially reluctant to invest the time required for a second meeting. Why can't this memo, like most memos, simply be delivered to the employee through the organization's regular transmission process, they ask. While this would be the most convenient approach, most companies that implement the Discipline Without Punishment system ask the manager to hold a short second meeting to review the memo with the employee.

While a second meeting does increase the total amount of time devoted to the Written Reminder transaction, that disadvantage is overcome by the benefits provided. First, managers actually conduct few Written Reminder transactions in the course of a year. Asking the manager to hold a second meeting to review the memo will not significantly increase his workload.

Second, the meeting is short and tightly focused—more than five minutes is too long. The sole purpose is to give the employee the memo, respond to any questions, and reconfirm the agreement that the problem will be solved.

This meeting may be one of the most important a manager can

Figure 6-2.   Written Reminder memo.

MEMORANDUM

To: Myra Thayer

From: Albert Hall

Date: April 30, 1995

Subject: Written Reminder

CC: John Webber, Production Manager
            Ellie Laurel, Personnel

Earlier today you and I met with John Webber to discuss your performance. I explained that this was a serious matter and that, because we had talked about your need to improve your performance several times in the past, we were issuing a formal Written Reminder.

The basic problem, Myra, is that while you do an excellent job in the actual selling part of your job, your performance is unacceptable in all of the support areas that are also part of your job requirements. Some of the examples we discussed include these:

1. About two weeks ago a customer returned a pair of hiking shoes that she had purchased three weeks before. While you could have processed the return and credit yourself, you told the customer that she would have to go to customer service in order to have the transaction completed. The customer reported to one of the customer service representatives that you had said you were too busy to take care of that when it appeared you were not busy at all.

2. You have been consistently late in sending your Record of Inventory summary to the accounting office.

3. When you are working the end-of-day schedule, you frequently leave merchandise in the wrong places and fail to leave your unit in such condition that the person working the start-of-day can immediately begin work the next morning.

Figure 6-2. Continued.

When you and I had our last conversation about this problem on February 22, at which time I issued you an Oral Reminder, you said that you understood the need to handle all parts of your job as effectively as you handle the selling part. Unfortunately, that has not happened and the problems we talked about earlier continue.

Myra, this situation is serious and must be immediately corrected. The failure to do so will lead to more serious disciplinary action and could result in your discharge from the company. As John and I explained during the meeting, no matter how good your sales are, if you cannot meet all of the job requirements we will be unable to keep you as an associate of the company.

I know that you can do as good a job in meeting the administrative and merchandising requirements as you do in meeting our selling expectations. You agreed that you would, and I look forward to your putting this problem behind you.

(signed) Albert Hall

have with a subordinate in terms of its ability to significantly influence performance. It gives the employee the opportunity to ask any questions that may have come up in the day or two since the initial meeting was held and allows the manager to explain the specific policy and procedural details of the Discipline Without Punishment process when the employee is likely to be less defensive. Most important, it provides an opportunity for the disciplinary documentation to be corrected if the manager has not accurately captured what was said during the meeting.

Should the Employee Sign?

In all of management, there is probably no piece of advice that is repeated unquestioningly more often than the admonition to always have the employee sign the document. Preprinted warning notice forms invariably contain a space for the employee's signature; every book that reviews the basic steps of the progressive-discipline procedure mandates that the employee be required to sign.

This is another area where the conventional wisdom about the discipline process is wrong.

Why do we ask the employee to sign? Managers invariably respond to that familiar question with a well-drilled schoolbook answer: "To acknowledge receipt."

But ask them when that acknowledgement of receipt will be valuable and they stumble. It takes some grappling to come up with the precise answer: In the event that the employee ever asserts that he did not see the document, his signature proves that he's lying.

When will that event ever arise? It turns out that in order for the employee's signature on the disciplinary documentation to have any value, the following scenario must play out in its entirety. The individual must continue his misbehavior through the point of a Decision Making Leave and then be fired. He must then challenge his termination through an arbitration or legal proceeding. The matter must then proceed to a formal hearing or trial without earlier settlement. At the trial or hearing the employee's sole defense must be that the incident never happened. The company, he must claim, is making it all up. It never happened: They put this in my file without telling me.

But this never happens. Only some of the people who get Written Reminders continue their misbehavior and move on to Decision Making Leaves. Most clean up their act and never encounter disciplinary problems again. Only some of the people who get Decision Making Leaves decide not to live up to their commitment and get terminated. Only some of those who get terminated take their unhappiness all the way to arbitration or a court proceeding.

And even then, a terminated employee rarely argues that the incident never happened and that management put the warning notice in his file when he wasn't looking. He argues instead that it was undeserved. "Oh yes, I got this thing," he will say, "but I shouldn't have. I didn't deserve it. They treated me differently than other people. They singled me out because I was black/female/handicapped/Jewish."

The only value that the employee's signature provides is the proof that the transaction did in fact take place. But employees almost never argue that it didn't take place, particularly because the supervisor is usually quite capable of testifying as to exactly what was said during the meeting and confirming that the discussion did in fact occur. Instead, they will acknowledge that they got the warning notice but that it was inappropriate or unfair, a much stronger argument than the mere pretense that the conversation never happened. The signature has no value.

"I have no problem with abolishing the preprinted warning notice and replacing it with the use of a memo directed to the employee," says Atlanta labor attorney Jim Wimberly. "While I have had employees deny that they have received certain warnings, I rarely, if ever, have had an employee deny that he received a memo directed to him for him to keep."

But ask managers what an employee's reaction is when you ask him to sign the warning notice. It just pisses him off, they'll tell you. Most of the time people refuse to sign.

And what do you do then?

They explain that when the employee refuses to sign, as he usually does, they write down that the employee refused to sign.

Your case is no stronger. Should the employee later claim that the transaction never happened, he will point out that the writing on the form saying that he refused to sign is certainly not his, and that not only did the company put it in his file without his knowing about it; they also wrote down that he refused to sign something that he had never seen.

Reflect on what happens when you ask the employee to sign the disciplinary documentation. At this point you have completed the Written Reminder discussion with the individual. Because you followed all of the procedures we have described, and because you dealt with that individual as a mature and responsible adult and conducted your discussion in a dignified and businesslike way, you have gained the employee's agreement to solve a problem. When you met with the employee and asked him to review the memo to make sure that it reasonably reflected the discussion that the two of you had, you again communicated your expectation that the problem was now a thing of the past. If you now present him with a pen and demand that he sign it, what are you saying to that person?

Sending Employees the Wrong Message

What the demand to sign the notice actually says to the employee is that you believe him to be a liar. The demand for his signature implies that even though he has agreed to solve the problem and correct the situation, he won't. You are suggesting that you are worried that he is going to continue his misbehavior and receive a Decision Making Leave, and that following the leave he will again perform unacceptably and be terminated. You are insinuating that you know that he will challenge the termination and that when the two of you are standing there, side by side, in front of the judge or arbitrator or hearing officer, he will lie about the fact that the two of you are talking about the problem right now. And therefore, your request proclaims, I am asking you to sign this form in order that I can protect myself against you.

Is that the message we want to send to the people who look to us for leadership?

I submit that it is not. I submit that there is a far more effective way to handle the issue of whether the employee should be required to sign the disciplinary notice. I propose that we abolish the progressive-discipline requirement that employees be compelled to sign the documentation.

What should we do? When the employee has read the memo and agreed that it basically reflects what was said in the meeting and then asks whether he now must sign it, I would have the manager look him in the eye and say, "John, are you a man of your word?"

I would have the manager wait until John replies that indeed he is.

"I know you are, John," I would have the manager respond. "So if you tell me that this problem is solved for good and we won't ever have to talk about it again, your word is good enough for me. You don't have to sign a thing."

Fanciful? Capricious? Perhaps. And while the scenario of the manager's looking John in the eye, asking him if he is indeed a man of his word, and then stating that his word is sufficient, may rarely be enacted verbatim, eliminating the worthless requirement that the manager compel John's signature will not lessen in the slightest the company's ability to defend its action in the rare case that the presence or absence of the signature ever becomes an issue. By breaking the traditional paradigm that we have followed for sixty years, we can dramatically raise the odds of both solving the problem completely and significantly strengthening the relationship.

Even when our experience with the individual suggests that we are dealing with someone who is unlikely to solve the problem and will not hesitate to lie if it serves his advantage, requiring the signature on the Written Reminder memo still provides little value. We still have the Decision Making Leave step in our arsenal. If there is any concern that the employee will not live up to his commitment following the Decision Making Leave and will prevaricate when asked about the history of events that resulted in his discharge, we may perhaps then decide to require the signature. But the better job we can do at putting the problem to rest at the Written Reminder stage, the less chance there is that the issue will ever escalate. And eliminating the signature requirement is one small but significant way.

7

Decision Making Leave

Of all the elements of Discipline Without Punishment, certainly the one that attracts the most attention is the final step of the system, the Decision Making Leave.

Managers who can comfortably accept the idea of dealing with employees who create problems as responsible adults during the first steps of the process are often reluctant to extend that same philosophy to the last step. The idea of a paid disciplinary suspension invariably takes some explaining.

As part of the initial development of Discipline Without Punishment, we explored all possible final-step strategies to find the one that would be most effective, not only in producing a change in the individual's behavior but also in providing a sufficiently clear and dramatic gesture that, should the individual's employment later have to be terminated because of continuing problems, would be seen as sufficient notice to the person that his job was at risk.

Other Alternatives

Probation?

We rejected the use of a probationary period because our experience showed that it was the least effective of all final-step strategies. In most cases, placing an employee on probation for ninety days was tantamount to avoiding dealing with the problem altogether. Neither the employee nor the supervisor really took it seriously. Most of the time it was an empty gesture that was aimed more at providing the appearance of action than in actually confronting the problem in a forthright way. Employees who had been placed on suspension usually felt that they had been given license by the organization to continue their misbehavior for another ninety days.

Performance Improvement Plans?

We were aware that some organizations had enjoyed a measure of success by increasing the counseling requirement that they expected of supervisors. When performance problems arose, their approach was to have the supervisor work jointly with the employee to create Performance Improvement Plans (PIPs). We liked the idea of supervisor and employee working together to develop action plans. We also saw several problems with this approach. First, it seemed to be appropriate only for those problems which fell into the performance category. Creating a PIP seemed like a ludicrous response when an employee decided to smoke in a restricted area or violated one of the other rules of the organization. PIPs for attendance issues seemed equally inappropriate.

Another problem we saw with using a PIP approach was that most of the activities required to create a PIP would already have been covered if the supervisor had been following the earlier requirements of being clear about exactly what the gap between desired and actual performance was, assessing whether that gap was caused by a lack of knowledge or a lack of execution, and then responding to the deficiency with either additional training or job engineering. If the supervisor had done all of that, he would have created a PIP in everything but name; if he had failed to do that, telling him to do it now as part of the discipline process would probably be ineffectual.

Finally, while the use of a Performance Improvement Plan could certainly be integrated with a more formal discipline procedure when it was appropriate (for example, when the problem involved an employee's deficiency in maintaining acceptable quantity or quality of production), the use of a PIP by itself was insufficient as a final discipline strategy. It failed to communicate in unmistakable terms the fact that the current situation was intolerable and that the consequence of failure to correct the problem would be the individual's termination.

A "Final Warning"?

Using a final warning as a last-step strategy had an important advantage over suspension: It meant not losing the employee's services during the time the individual would have been away on suspension. Avoiding suspension obviously meant avoiding disrupting the production schedule as other employees were redeployed to cover for the absence. On the other hand, we realized that earlier warnings to this individual about the need for change had not been successful. What evidence did we have, we asked, that more of the same would be any different. (One manager related the unusual experience he had once had in giving an employee a final warning. When he told the employee that this was a final warning and that he wasn't going to talk to the employee about the problem again, the employee responded that he was glad the manager wasn't going to talk about it anymore because he was getting tired of listening to the manager's complaints.)

The use of a final warning failed to meet another of our criteria. We realized that at the final step of the discipline procedure we needed a dramatic gesture that would unmistakably communicate to the individual that we were serious about the fact that the situation could not continue. Only a suspension from work could prove, not just to the employee himself but also to any third party who might later review our actions, that the end of the road had at last been reached.

A Tough-Minded Approach

When the possibility of using a paid disciplinary suspension was first suggested, most managers ridiculed the idea. It's a soft approach, they said. We need a tough-minded solution to the serious problems this plant is facing. As we explored the idea, however, we soon realized that it was the traditional unpaid suspension that was in fact excessively soft and tender-minded.

Our reasoning went like this. The traditional disciplinary layoff without pay was certainly punishing. But was it a genuinely tough-minded and uncompromising response to an employee's unacceptable behavior?

While an suspension without pay was certainly distasteful for both the supervisor and the employee, we realized that the organization asked almost nothing of the employee except that he serve out his time and not get caught repeating the misbehavior.

Now, however, although the individual was being paid for the time he was away from work, he was also being held to a far higher standard. Returning to work was no longer merely a matter of serving out his sentence. In spite of the pay, he now was confronted with a far tougher company response to his failure to meet standards. In order to return to his job he had to make an active decision to commit to fully acceptable performance and advise his boss that that was the decision he had made.

Just serving one's time, while somewhat embarrassing and perhaps financially taxing, was not particularly demanding. But to have to spend a day thinking about one's future and then stand in front of one's boss and commit to fully acceptable performance—now there was a tough response.

Decision Making Leave Procedures

The following subsections discuss how to handle all aspects of the Decision Making Leave effectively.

Before the Meeting

As in the previous steps of the system, once the supervisor determines that the final step of the Discipline Without Punishment process is appropriate, he completes the analysis of actual and desired performance, the adverse effects of the problem, and the logical consequences if the employee fails to change. At this point, since the Decision Making Leave is the final step of the system, the most significant consequence is, of course, termination.

Every organization that has adopted Discipline Without Punishment requires approval by both a senior line manager and the head of the human resources function before the step is initiated. If a single serious incident precipitates the Decision Making Leave, the supervisor should advise the employee at the time of the incident that this is a serious situation and they will need to discuss it. Since senior management has not yet reviewed and approved the Decision Making Leave, he should advise the individual that he will let him know when they will meet. If the employee can continue to work without presenting any risk to the organization or fellow workers, he may be allowed to continue working while the deliberation process is completed. If there is risk present, he should be suspended pending investigation and told that he will be advised when to return.

More often the precipitating event is not a single calamitous outburst of misbehavior. Instead it is a final straw in a continuing series of minor failures to meet the company's expectations following the Written Reminder. In this case the supervisor, aware that a Decision Making Leave may be forthcoming, has the time to discuss the anticipated need to take the final step with senior members of the organization.

Having secured the necessary approvals, the supervisor must determine how he will cover the employee's work while the individual is away on the leave. In some cases it will be merely a matter of a minor backlog accumulating; in other cases a major revision to the work schedule may be necessary.

Scheduling the Leave

To what extent should the timing of the leave be adjusted to fit the convenience of the organization? Two guidelines apply here: first, the employee's absence on Decision Making Leave should result in as little organizational disruption as possible. Second, the leave should occur as soon as possible after the precipitating event.

Most of the time the incident that causes the organization to decide to impose a DML and the beginning of the leave itself will occur on the same day. The employee commits the culminating offense, the supervisor rounds up the necessary approvals and plans for work coverage, and by the end of the day the supervisor holds the conversation with the employee and then sends him home to think it over.

Sometimes organizations aren't that lucky. It may be that there is serious deliberation required to determine whether the employee's actions do in fact merit moving to the final step. This is particularly true when several employees have been involved in a minor incident of misbehavior, especially when one is already on an active level of disciplinary action. Determining the wisest approach in this case may require several heads to sleep on it overnight.

A more difficult decision arises when the need for a DML is clear but the timing is impossible. If Sally, who last week received a Written Reminder for smoking in a restricted area, is again seen smoking in the same place, the appropriateness of a DML is unarguable. But this week is annual inventory, and Sally is the only inventory clerk who understands the whole system and can serve as a trainer to others.

One approach would be to bite the bullet and place Sally on Decision Making Leave immediately, recognizing that somehow the organization would find a way to deal with her absence if she happened to call in sick that day (and at least this way there is a little forewarning). Alternatively the supervisor could have the conversation with Sally and advise her that she will be placed on a Decision Making Leave on _____ (the first workable day that her presence can be spared).

Is the Decision Making Leave a Benefit?

A separate issue involves scheduling the DML day to avoid making the day an apparent benefit for the employee. This concern arises when an employee commits an offense that triggers the supervisor's decision to place the employee on a DML. But it's Thursday morning, the supervisor frets. If I place him on Decision Making Leave now, he's not only going to have this afternoon off free, but a long weekend as well. Should I juggle the Decision Making Leave transaction in order to prevent the DML day from being part of a weekend?

In a word, no.

Behind this question is the lingering remnant of the delusion that somehow the Decision Making Leave is a form of reward. What the person who asks this question fails to realize is that if the DML day happens to abut a weekend its impact is even greater. Instead of having only one day where the employee's thoughts will be concentrated on the upcoming meeting where the decision to stay or quit will have to be announced, the individual now faces three days under the gun. The Decision Making Leave is not an additional paid holiday. A Tampa Electric Company employee who returned from Decision Making Leave commented, "Believe me, brother, that was no vacation!"

The only workable way to schedule the DML is to hold the meeting as soon as possible following the triggering incident. As soon as the meeting is over, the employee leaves the premises and is on Decision Making Leave, at full pay, for the balance of that day and for the next regularly scheduled workday. If that day happens to abut a weekend, so be it. Only if the day abuts an employee's regularly scheduled vacation would it be wise to consciously reschedule the day, not because the DML would extend the employee's vacation but, out of charity and compassion, to eliminate the anxiety that a two-week-long Decision Making Leave would produce!

Having secured all necessary approvals and arranged the work schedule so that the employee's absence on DML will cause the minimum disruption possible, the manager can make the final arrangements for the meeting. This will include reviewing the notes and documentation from the previous Oral and Written Reminders, arranging for an appropriate location to hold the meeting, and arranging for any required witnesses or employee representative.

During the Meeting

The initial part of the meeting follows the same pattern as the earlier Oral and Written Reminder discussions. The manager opens the meeting by describing specifically the issue that has caused the need for the discussion. He listens to what the employee has to say to confirm that there is no unknown reason for the Decision Making Leave transaction not to take place.

Having confirmed that a Decision Making Leave is appropriate, the manager explains the procedural elements of the Decision Making Leave in detail to make sure that there is no question or confusion on the employee's part.

The manager begins by telling the employee that he or she is being placed on a Decision Making Leave, the final step of the company's disciplinary procedures. He advises the individual that immediately upon the conclusion of this meeting, the employee is to leave company premises for the rest of the day. He is told that he is being suspended from work on the following day and that he is to remain at home making a final decision about whether or not he can abide by company standards.

He is told that this day is to be used to make a decision about his job once and for all: either to solve the immediate problem and make a total commitment to good performance in every area of the job, or decide that working here is not for him and return with a decision to quit and find more satisfying employment somewhere else.

The employee should be advised that while the company will pay him for the day he is out, he must understand precisely what the company's expectations of him are and exactly where he stands. He is not simply to return to work on the day after his leave but must return with a final decision that he can live up to: to solve the problem forever and never create another situation that requires disciplinary action, or resign. He needs to be told that the reason the company is paying him is to indicate that the organization does hope that he will decide to change and stay, but that another problem that requires disciplinary action will result in his termination.

The employee should be advised exactly when he is due back (the beginning of his regularly scheduled work shift on the day following the Decision Making Leave) and what to do when he does return (come into the manager's office and advise his boss of the decision he has made).

More than in any other disciplinary transaction, it is critical here that the employee confirm that he knows exactly what is expected and that there are no questions about exactly what he is to do.

Unlike previous conversations where the employee did most of the talking, now it is the manager who talks the most. The employee's responsibility is less to discuss the problem than it is to confirm his understanding of exactly what the company is instructing him to do. There is actually little real discussion that needs to take place at this point. Unless the situation represents such a grave violation that the company has moved directly to the Decision Making Leave, bypassing all initial steps, the problem has usually been talked to excess at this point. Over and over the employee and manager have discussed the employee's failure to meet the company's standards, the employee has agreed to improve and meet at least the minimum standard of acceptable performance, and has consistently failed to live up to his promise. The time for exploring various alternative approaches and training possibilities has passed.

The issue is now a straightforward matter of the employee's need to make a decision: Will he do what the company is paying him to do, or will he not? The company is now demanding, once and for all, that he make that a formal, conscious decision—one that he is prepared to live up to in the future, with expulsion from the organizational family the consequence if he fails. Other than clearly communicating that message, there is little else that needs to be said:

Manager:	. . . Gerry, when we had both the Oral Reminder and Written Reminder conversations, you agreed that you would solve this problem and perform your job in an acceptable manner. That hasn't happened. This morning the same problem came up again.
Employee:	Yeah, well, I tried, but sometimes things happen.
Manager:	Gerry, you really have to make a decision now about whether this really is the right job for you.
Employee:	Oh, yeah. Of course it is. I like working here.
Manager:	I'm glad to hear you say that, Gerry, but this problem keeps coming up. You really must make a serious decision about whether you can in fact solve this problem and meet all of the job requirements. That's why at the end of this meeting you will be placed on Decision Making Leave.
Employee:	You're gonna fire me?
Manager:	No, Gerry. You're not being fired. You are being placed on Decision Making Leave, the final step of our discipline procedure. You are being suspended from work tomorrow. I want you to spend tomorrow thinking through whether this is the right job for you and whether you can solve this problem and perform every part of your job at a fully acceptable level.
Employee:	I don't need tomorrow off. I can tell you right now that I want my job.
Manager:	I want you to make that a real decision, Gerry. We are

past the point of quick commitments that you don't live up to. That's why you will be out tomorrow. I want you to use your time tomorrow deciding either to solve this problem forever and make a commitment to fully acceptable performance in every area of your job, or decide to quit and get a job that's better for you.

Employee: This job is fine with me. I can tell you right now what my decision will be.

Manager: It isn't enough just to decide that you want to keep your job. Let me be real clear on exactly what you've got to do. Gerry, you can decide one of two things. You can decide that you will solve this problem and that you will also commit yourself to doing your job so that there will never be any further problems—either this one or any other. Or you can decide to quit. Is the decision you've got to make, clear?

Employee: Yeah. You want me to promise to do a good job.

Manager: No, Gerry, that's not it. You've made us that promise before and you haven't lived up to it. Sorry, but that's the way it is.

Now it requires more than that. When you come back the day after tomorrow I want you to come into my office and let me know what you have decided. It can be either to solve this problem plus agree to do every part of your job acceptably, or tell me that you're quitting. I can live with either choice, but you've got to make the decision.

Employee: OK . . . I can shape up or ship out.

Manager: That's right. I hope you do decide to change and stay with us. To indicate that we're serious about wanting to keep you on the team, you'll get full pay for the time you're out. We're not going to punish you or treat you like a little kid who's been naughty. You're an adult and you've got to accept adult responsibilities.

Employee: So I'll get paid for tomorrow?

Manager: Yes. I don't want you to worry about your pay. I want you to concentrate on thinking about your job and whether you can do it right. Let me make sure you understand, Gerry. While I do hope that you decide to change and stay with us, if another problem comes up

	that requires disciplinary action, you can expect to be terminated.
Employee:	So if I do this again I'll get fired.
Manager:	Yes. But it's more than that. We are past the point of asking you just to solve this one problem. If you want to keep your job, Gerry, what you have to do is make a total commitment to good performance in every part of your job. That's because if another disciplinary problem comes up, this one or any other, I'll recommend that you be discharged.
Employee:	That's not fair!
Manager:	What's not fair?
Employee:	Expecting me agree to do every part of my job perfectly. I'm not perfect. Nobody's perfect. You're just setting a trap to fire me.
Manager:	I'm not asking you to be perfect. But I am telling you that we are at the last step of our discipline procedure, and if you want to keep your job you have to perform in a totally acceptable way. You must understand, Gerry, that if any other problem that requires disciplinary action arises, you can expect to be terminated. But I believe that if you think about it tomorrow, and decide to make a genuine change, you will be able to live up to it. You had a solid record for several years before this problem got started. . . . I believe that you could get back to that if you tried.
Employee:	Well, OK, but I really don't need a day off.
Manager:	It's not an option, Gerry. We need you to understand exactly how serious this situation really is. This is the final step of the discipline procedure. You will be out tomorrow; you must be back in here first thing Wednesday morning with your final decision.
Employee:	OK. I'll see you then.
Manager:	Come on, I'll walk out with you.

Based on the manager's experience with the individual and the way the employee acts during the meeting, the manager may decide to escort the person off the premises. As we see in the above case, while the manager was communicating a friendly closure to the meeting, he was also making sure that the employee immediately left company premises and reduced the risks of any inappropriate behaviors while the employee was leaving.

No formal documentation of the incident can take place until the employee returns with his decision. It is important for the manager to make some immediate notes about any important statements or actions on the employee's part during the meeting, but the manager's primary responsibility between the start and the completion of the leave is to make sure that the employee's work gets done.

When the Employee Returns

Most organizations that have implemented the Discipline Without Punishment system report that the employee is usually waiting for the manager on the morning following the day of the Decision Making Leave. People do take it seriously. While cynics may scoff at giving people a "vacation day," and managers may be concerned about the appearance of rewarding bad behavior, almost universally the individuals who receive a Decision Making Leave treat it very seriously indeed. Not all of them live up to the commitments they make, but few return with a casual response.

One of the supervisors at a New England General Electric plant I had worked with described the experience he had in placing one of his employees on a Decision Making Leave. He described how angry the employee had been when she had left the plant. Because he expected the same belligerence when she returned following the leave, he was surprised when she came back subdued, almost meek. In a quiet, almost apologetic way she told him that she had thought it over and would like to keep her job and would not create any further problems and would it be all right if she went back to work now?

She went back to work and immediately began performing exactly as expected. For a few days she was reserved and a little remote, but gradually the dampening effects of the Decision Making Leave wore off and she resumed her normal disposition, continuing to maintain a fully acceptable record.

About two months went by. Her work record, if perhaps not excellent, was certainly completely acceptable, and her mood had brightened to the point where she was always pleasant to be around. The supervisor became very curious. He related:

I couldn't stand it anymore. I had to know what had happened during her Decision Making Leave that produced such a transformation. So one day when it was just the two of us talking, I said to her, "Becky, I know this is none of my business and you can tell me to get lost if you don't want to respond. But I just have to ask you something. Ever since the day after that Decision Making Leave, when you came back and told me that you were going to change, you really have changed. What happened to you when you were on Decision Making Leave?"

She paused and got serious for a moment; then she said, "Well, I will tell you. When you put me on that leave, pardon my French, but I was pissed. I didn't think I deserved it and I knew I wasn't going to do one thing different from what I had been doing—you could do whatever you wanted about it.

"When I got up the next morning, I was still angry, but I decided that I'd just put the day to good use and get some things done that I don't have time for on the weekends. I got my kids off to school, got a cup of coffee, and then sat down with the paper to see if there were any sales.

"As I was going through the paper I started thinking about why it was that I was sitting here getting ready to go shopping on a Tuesday when everybody I knew was at work. I kept on thinking about what you had said and thinking about my job, and when my kids got home from school that afternoon I was still at the kitchen table."

It doesn't happen that way for everyone. Not all employees will come back from a Decision Making Leave with the same transformation that this woman demonstrated. But it does happen.

With surprising consistency managers report that people that they did not expect to respond as adults actually take personal responsibility for their own behavior when they are required to. In the frequent number of cases where this does occur, managers also report that the relationship between themselves and the individual is strengthened. After the immediate emotional upheaval created by the Decision Making Leave has calmed and some time has passed, it is not uncommon for the employee to view the manager as that stern coach most of us admire—the one who holds us to a high standard but expresses enough confidence in us that we stay in the game when we are otherwise ready to quit.

Not everyone is transformed. Some come back with glowing words about how they have seen the light and will sin no more but quickly return to their former ways and are terminated. Some return no more willing to take personal responsibility than they were when they left, seeing their problems as simply the result of fate or chance or a run of bad luck. They may perform badly enough to be discharged or just well enough to hang on, but they never move up much from the bottom of the pile.

In a very few cases, the employee votes with his feet and never shows up again.

In even fewer cases does the employee return and announce his resignation from the company. The Decision Making Leave causes many people to decide to change employers, but they see little value in precipitously resigning. They return, they perform sufficiently well to maintain membership in the family (and frequently they perform extremely well, concerned about the quality of reference they will receive), and within a few weeks or months find a new employer where they can get a fresh start. In almost every one of these cases, the decision turns out to be the best outcome for all.

But how do the results of the Decision Making Leave compare with the traditional unpaid disciplinary layoff as a final-step strategy? Without exception, managers report that the use of the Decision Making Leave produces two significant advantages over the previous system:

1. More people actually do change, return to fully acceptable performance, and maintain that correction for a significant period of time.
2. The few people who continue to perform unacceptably following the DML are terminated with far less guilt and hesitation, and those terminations stick.

Managers who see the approach as feeble or soft when they first encounter it usually become advocates once they see the results. After the system had been in effect for a year, Tampa Electric surveyed exactly one hundred of their managers in the departments that were using it on a pilot basis. All but two not only agreed that the program should be continued but recommended its expansion. "When you get 98 out of 100 managers agreeing on anything," one senior executive observed, "you know you've got something that's very successful."

As soon as the employee arrives at work on the day after the leave, he should, as previously instructed, come into his boss's office and announce the decision he has made. This is a serious event and should be treated as such by both parties. There is only benefit to be gained by treating this occasion thoughtfully. Even a note of solemnity would not be out of place. Both the manager's words and demeanor should communicate that the organization considers this to be a recommitment to the standards that were accepted when the employee was first engaged. A cavalier, "Yeah, boss, I've thought it over and I've decided to stay," would be entirely inappropriate, and all of the manager's actions and behaviors should indicate that very serious business is at hand.

The supervisor may need to coach the employee to get the full commitment stated:

Manager:	I'm glad to see you, Gerry. What decision have you made?
Employee:	Well, like I told you when I left, I really do want my job.
Manager:	And?
Employee:	And I'm going to do it right.
Manager:	And?
Employee:	Whattayamean, "and"? Isn't that enough?
Manager:	Gerry, I was very clear with you before you left exactly the decision you needed to make if you want to continue to work here. You have to decide not only that you want the job, but that you will solve the specific problem that we talked about and will do your job in a fully acceptable way.
Employee:	Well, sure, that's what I meant.
Manager:	So what is your decision?
Employee:	Do I need to spell it out for you?

Manager: Yes, Gerry, you do. I need to know exactly what your decision is.

Employee: Robert, I have decided that I do want to keep my job. I will solve the problem. I will do my job right. Is that OK?

Manager: Gerry, do you really mean it?

Employee: Yeah, Robert, I really do. I really did do a lot of thinking and I'm sorry about this whole thing. As you said, we are never going to have to talk about this again.

At this point, the employee's decision is clear. The agreement has been reached. But this is the final step of the discipline procedure, and the employee also has the right to know what the failure to live up to his good intentions will involve:

Manager: Gerry, I'm glad that you made that choice. I was hoping that you would because you're a valuable part of this team and I don't want to lose you.

Employee: Thanks.

Manager: But you do need to know where you stand. This is the last step of the company's Discipline Without Punishment system. There aren't any more chances after this. If another problem comes up—this one or anything else, whatever it may be—that requires disciplinary action, you can expect that you will be terminated. I don't want that to happen, you don't want that to happen, and I need your commitment that it's never going to happen.

Employee: Robert, you've got it. Believe me, we are never going to talk about this or anything like it again.

The employee has now been advised of the future consequences if this or any other problem arises. It is now time for the manager to wrap things up:

Manager: Gerry, I'm glad you have made this decision, and quite honestly I believe that we will never have to talk about it again. Since this is the final step of our discipline procedure, as soon as this meeting is over I will be writing you a memo confirming our conversation and your agreement to solve this problem and perform acceptably in every area of your job. In that memo, Gerry I will also be advis-

Employee:	ing you again of what I just said: that if any further problems come up that require disciplinary action, the logical consequence is termination.
Employee:	Don't rub it in.
Manager:	That's not my intent. I do need to make it really clear.
Employee:	It's clear.
Manager:	But you also know that this is active for eighteen months. You live up to your commitment, this comes out of your file.
Employee:	I can do that.
Manager:	I know you can, Gerry. Now let's get back to work and put this behind us.

With that, the employee leaves. The only things left for the manager to do are to document the Decision Making Leave transaction and then to monitor the employee's performance to make sure that the problem once solved, stays solved.

Documenting the Decision Making Leave

The documentation requirements for the Decision Making Leave are virtually the same as those for the Written Reminder. The specific details of the problem need to be recorded, the complete history of any earlier discussions about the situation, and, most important, a record of the exact agreement the employee made and a statement of the consequences to follow if the agreement is not maintained.

After the memo has been prepared, it should be reviewed in a brief meeting with the employee. The individual should be asked to confirm that the memo reasonably reflects the content of the discussions between himself and the manager and, more important, the agreement that the employee made as a result of the Decision making Leave. The manager's positive expectation of change and correction should also be communicated, as well as a final restatement of the fact that any further problems will logically result in termination.

Should the employee be required to sign the memo to acknowledge receipt? While the chances that the signature will ever be useful are slight, there may, at this final step, be more value in requesting the signature than there was at the Written Reminder stage.

At the time of the Written Reminder, the organization still had the Decision Making Leave in its arsenal if the employee did not live up to the agreement he had made. At the point of Decision Making Leave, there is no further disciplinary step available. If the employee fails to perform acceptably, he will be terminated. There may be value in emphasizing the importance of the commitment by asking for a signature, not merely to acknowledge receipt of the memo, but to affirm positively the commitment to perform acceptably in the future.

Figure 7-1 is a sample of a memo documenting a Decision Making Leave transaction.

Common Questions about the Decision Making Leave

Both in the explaining of the Decision Making Leave to the senior executives of a company that is considering adopting Discipline Without Punishment and in the reviewing of the rationale for the procedure during the management training programs, a great many questions about the step arise. Here are some of the more predictable questions about the Decision Making Leave step and their answers.

Q. *What do we do if the employee causes another problem after the Decision Making Leave?*

A. Fire him.

Q. *Yeahbut what if a lot of time has gone by and he really has almost completely shaped up and the problem is a little different from the one that earned him the DML and I'm not sure that my boss will back me up and I really don't want to fire him anyway?*

A. Don't fire him.

Q. *How do I decide which to do?*

A. Good question. When the employee returns from Decision Making Leave it is critical that he be advised that this is the final step of the company's discipline procedure and that any further problems, of any kind, will be met by termination. Whether you actually will terminate will depend on several factors, including how long it has been since the Decision Making Leave took place, the specific viola-

Figure 7-1.   Memo documenting Decision Making Leave.

MEMORANDUM

To: Gerry Borland

From: Robert Quadro

Date: June 29, 1995

Subject: Decision Making Leave

CC: Cyril Burt, Production Manager
           Cecille Nostramus, Vice President, Operations
           Julie Hewitt, Vice President, Human Resources

You were placed on a Decision Making Leave on June 28, 1995, because of your failure to perform and record all safety checks before certifying that the equipment for which you were responsible was ready for shipment.

This problem was initially brought to your attention in several informal discussions you and I had earlier this year. When the problem continued, you received a formal Oral Reminder, the first step of our discipline procedure, on April 21, 1995. Later, you received a Written Reminder, the second step of our discipline procedure, on May 14. In each of these conversations I reviewed exactly what our expectations were and you agreed that you would follow them. When the same problem arose earlier this week I reviewed the situation with Mr. Burt, Ms. Nostramus and Ms. Hewitt and we agreed that a Decision-Making Leave, the final step of our discipline policy, was appropriate.

I advised you that this was the final step of our discipline procedure and that you were to make a final decision: either to solve the problem of performing and recording all safety checks and, in addition, to commit to fully acceptable performance in every area of your job, or to quit. When you returned from the leave you told me that you wanted to continue your employment and that you would solve the problem and would perform every part of your job in a fully acceptable manner.

Figure 7-1. Continued.

As I advised you during our meeting, you must immediately correct this situation. In addition, you must maintain fully acceptable performance in every area of your job, whether related to this issue or not, since any further problems that require disciplinary action will result in your termination.

(signed) Robert Quadro

tion that occurred, how the employee's overall performance has been, what you have done with other people who have committed similar infractions, etc.

In making the decision to terminate, however, there, is a third goal besides the two unchanging goals of solving the problem and enhancing the relationship: maintaining the integrity of the system. If employees discover that problems following a Decision Making Leave are ignored by a lily-livered management staff that is unwilling to terminate people who fail to perform at the minimum acceptable level, the overall performance of the organization is likely to decline drastically. Highly motivated and committed performers become discouraged when they discover that the organization condones irresponsibility on the part of both the leaders and the led. Sluggards and organizational ne'er-do-wells will revel in this laissez-faire atmosphere where little is demanded and less is produced. They will attract their shiftless and indolent comrades to apply for a position in a company where their sloth will be tolerated.

When problems arise after a Decision Making Leave, our human compassion may tempt us to give the employee a second chance. But is it a "second chance" we are actually providing? Most people in any company never create disciplinary problems. The few who do, usually clean up their act after an Oral Reminder. The few who do not, usually shape up after receiving a Written Reminder. The few who still do not, usually come to their senses when they preview unemployment on a Decision Making Leave. So the tiny few who do not perform at the minimum level tolerable following the Decision Making Leave step are not asking for a second chance. Having had a second chance, and a third, and a fourth, they plead for a fifth. In the absence of gravely mitigating circumstances it is time to say, "Enough's enough," cut your losses, and hire a replacement who will appreciate employment with your organization.

As a weathered manager once said, "When in doubt, throw 'em out."

Q. *If the employee continues to create problems after a Decision Making Leave, would it be advisable to try a more traditional step like an unpaid layoff of several days?*

A. No. First, moving to a punitive response will vitiate the integrity of the system. It will communicate to all that management only talks about dealing with employees as mature and responsible adults, but when push comes to shove, they still deal with them as children.

Second, it increases the probability that employees who are finally terminated from the organization will be returned if they appeal their discharge. The arbitrator or hearing officer, upon discovering that the organization's unofficial but actual discipline policy (as opposed to the one officially stated in the policy manual) provides for an unpaid layoff of perhaps three days after an employee has received a Decision Making Leave, might order a terminated employee reinstated but with an unpaid layoff of perhaps five days this time. But if the organization can demonstrate that it consistently has given people a fair chance to get problems solved through a series of increasingly progressive but nonpunitive steps and then terminates anyone who fails to perform acceptably after the final step, the chances that an outside third party would force the company to take the employee back are much smaller.

One large manufacturing organization has compiled an enviable record of success with third-party challenges by always explaining completely the Discipline Without Punishment system that they use. Their review includes the complete mechanics of the system, the underlying philosophy, and the training their supervisors receive. Their attorney then explains to the judge or arbitrator that they recognize that it is possible that in any given case they may have erred and erroneously terminated someone who was unworthy of being discharged. In that case, the attorney explains, that person will be brought back and made whole. Then the attorney states that they will not, under any circumstances, violate the nonpunitive approach they have adopted. If ordered to return an employee whom they have terminated they will only do so by paying the person for the full amount of lost wages, even if the arbitrator or agency finds guilt on both sides and orders the employee reinstated without back pay. They report that the rare times when they have been required to reinstate a terminated employee have occurred only when there were serious questions about whether the termination was justified.

Q. *What if he says he will change but I know that he won't?*

A. Don't be too sure. Many managers have reported that they have been surprised at the power of the Decision Making Leave to command the attention of an otherwise recalcitrant individual who has scorned lesser attempts to convince him to modify his behavior. The combination of the dramatic gesture of the disciplinary suspension plus the unexpected demonstration of good faith and fair dealing on the organization's part has convinced many individuals to correct what was considered a hopeless situation.

On the other hand, naïveté is not a virtue. Be sure to monitor closely the performance of every employee who returns from Decision Making Leave. In those cases where you are suspicious that the agreement is cavalier, pay even closer attention.

Q. *What if the employee is late getting back from DML or calls in asking for more time?*

A. If the employee calls in asking for more time, refuse the request and demand that he return immediately at the beginning of his next scheduled work shift with his answer.

If the employee is late, ask why. Unless there are powerfully mitigating circumstances, the wisest course would be to terminate the person for failure to return from leave as scheduled.

If an individual calls in "sick" or presents some other excuse for failure to return as scheduled, termination is probably the appropriate course.

In each of these cases we are not dealing with the average employee of the organization. We are not even dealing with the average problem employee. We are dealing with the problem employee who has completely lost control of his ability to act rationally and in his own obvious best interests. He is standing on the precipice of termination waiting to see if we will rush to his rescue and pull him back from the abyss.

Do not rush. Let him fall.

Q. *Are there any employees for whom a Decision Making Leave is not appropriate?*

A. The only employees for whom a Decision Making Leave would not be appropriate would be those whose commitment to the enterprise is irrelevant and unnecessary. It might, perhaps, be unnecessary to give a Decision Making Leave to a seasonal worker when most of the season's work is complete. But in any organization where a continuing high standard of performance and a high degree of organizational commitment is important, the Decision Making Leave is appropriate.

One advantage that the Decision Making Leave has over all other final-step disciplinary strategies is that it is appropriate for use at higher organizational levels. It would be considered most irregular to tell a vice president that he was being placed on probation or to give a senior scientist a three-day unpaid suspension. But both of these individuals could be given a Decision Making Leave with powerful effect. Since both are exempt employees the issue of pay for the day is irrelevant, but the effect of being refused admission to the premises for one day and compelled to reconsider one's commitment to the enterprise would be both dignified and fitting.

In one large West Coast organization, the very first individual to receive a Decision Making Leave was the organization's director of labor relations. From the moment the agency head decided to implement a nonpunitive approach, this old-school tough bargainer vocally opposed the decision, in spite of the support of the senior management group and his boss, the vice president of human resources. The day after implementation, the VP–HR called the director of labor relations into his office and told him that he was to spend the following day at home thinking about whether he could actually do his job under the new philosophy that the organization was embracing or whether it would be better for him to find another agency where his adversarial and antagonistic approach to dealing with bargaining unit employees would still be tolerated. "But it won't be tolerated here," his boss told him. "Come back the day after tomorrow and let me know what your decision is." He returned chastened, got on board, and after a few months of experience in seeing how the nonpunitive approach was indeed a tougher response than the punitive system he had been using for years, became an advocate.

Q. *What if the employee refuses to make any decision at all?*

A. This question invariably comes up in explaining the approach to managers in implementation seminars. "What do I do," one will ask, "if the guy just stands there when he comes back and tells me that he ain't gonna quit and he ain't gonna agree to nothin'?"

Begin by recognizing that we are dealing with a disturbed individual. It is extremely rare for someone to return from a Decision Making Leave and refuse to agree.

Let us be blunt about what it is that we are asking the employee to agree to do. We are not asking him to perform at a superior level or even at a mediocre level. All that we are asking is that he agree not to create any problems which will provoke his termination; that he agree to perform at any level above that of unacceptability. Our demands of him could not be lower. If he is unable or unwilling to agree to solve a problem which has caused him to arrive at the company's final disciplinary step, and refuses further to agree to perform his job at the minimum level of acceptability, we do not need his services.

If the employee is represented by a shop steward or other union representative, it may be appropriate to give the representative and the individual a few minutes alone so that the steward can explain the serious predicament he is causing for himself. Otherwise, tell him bluntly that his response is unacceptable, that he must either decide to correct the problem or announce that he is quitting, and the company will consider his failure to respond appropriately to be an act of insubordination for which termination is the proper remedy. Unless an immediate response of commitment to acceptable performance is received, most organizations would suspend the person pending investigation, then subsequently decide to terminate for insubordination.

Q. *What if the employee never returns?*

A. First, make an immediate attempt to determine whether he has involuntarily been prevented from returning by an accident or emergency. Almost all individuals return promptly following a Decision Making Leave. Supervisors regularly report that they find the individual there waiting for them when they arrive on the morning they are due back.

If the individual simply does not return, most organizations provide that three days of "no-call, no-show" constitutes job abandonment and terminate the individual for that reason.

Q. *What if the person comes back while he's supposed to be on Decision Making Leave and starts to work?*

A. It happens more than you would think.

The fact that employees frequently show up for work when they are supposed to be away on Decision Making Leave strongly refutes the misconception that they will not take the step seriously but will intentionally misbehave in order to get another vacation day.

As soon as the manager sees the employee he should tell him to stop working and direct him to come into the manager's office or some other private area. Ask the employee what he is doing. In most cases, the individual is so embarrassed by having been placed on the Decision Making Leave that he is dealing with his feelings through denial. While we may sympathize with the person, the choice is not his to make. Tell him that this is a formal disciplinary step and that he is to leave immediately and return on the following day with his decision.

Unless there was any more to the incident than a misunderstanding or the individual's attempt to deny the reality of the step, do not make any further reference to the event and let it go as a misunderstanding.

Q. *What do I say if other employees ask, "Where's Harry?"*

A. Say, "Harry's out today." If they continue to ask, tell them that that is Harry's business and that just as you would honor and respect their privacy, so you honor and respect his.

Very early in the course of implementing the Discipline Without Punishment system with organizations I discovered another difference between the nonpunitive approach and the traditional system. When employees returned from a three-day unpaid disciplinary layoff, most would attempt to save face by bragging about how good it was to get away for a while and how they wished that their suspension could have been longer. We discovered after implementing Discipline Without Punishment that just the opposite was happening. Employees who received DMLs returned to work subdued and reticent about what had transpired. "You were out yesterday," a co-worker would say. "Yes, I was," the individual would respond, and turn back to his duties eager to terminate the conversation.

Q. *What do I do if the employee says he can decide during the Decision Making Leave meeting? Can I accept his decision on the spot?*

A. No. The employee will frequently offer a decision immediately upon being advised of the Decision Making Leave in order to avoid having to spend the day away from work (again rebutting the notion that the Decision Making Leave rewards bad behavior). He sounds so contrite and sincere that the manager is convinced that finally the message has gotten through and the problem will now be solved. It is tempting to accept the employee's decision on the spot and process the paperwork as though the DML had actually occurred or to reflect that the employee's decision was accepted in lieu of his spending the day away from work on the DML.

This is invariably a bad idea.

As sincere as the individual may sound, this will turn out to be the case where the employee will continue his mischief and receive a well-earned discharge. But when he goes to court or arbitration, as invariably these types do, his defense will be that the company did not follow its own policies in terminating him.

"Everybody else got a day off to think about it," he will whimper. "But not me. I had to make the decision without the chance to reflect for a day that all the others were given."

"Wait a minute!" you will respond. "Yes, he made his decision right on the spot, but that's because he begged us to let him do it. He pleaded with us not to send him home."

"I don't recall that," he will coyly say. "All I know is that everybody else got a day with pay to make a final decision, and my decision was made right while I was on the carpet."

Q. *Is it fair to ask for a "total-performance commitment"?*

A. The most meaningful difference between the Decision Making Leave and the traditional unpaid disciplinary suspension is not that the employee is paid for the period he is away from work while on a DML. That is the most obvious difference, but not the most important.

The most important difference between the two final-step strategies lies in what the organization asks of the individual who reaches this point. The traditional approach asks nothing more of the employee than that he serve out his time. When the unpaid suspension period has been completed, the employee typically returns to his workplace and picks up his hammer where he had put it down. He may be reprimanded for what he has done, he may be warned that if he does it again he will be fired, but he is not required to make any affirmative commitment to the organization or any positive resolution regarding his future behavior.

The Decision Making Leave rejects the traditional approach, not only because it is punishing but because it is insufficiently demanding. Now the employee must do more than amuse himself for the three days that he is off the payroll. Now he must stand before his boss and announce his decision, with whatever level of sincerity he can muster, about his future as a member of the organizational family. And the commitment he is being asked for is not merely a commitment to solve the immediate problem that triggered the Decision Making Leave, but the commitment to totally acceptable performance in every area of his job.

8

Discharge

Most people who are placed on a Decision Making Leave return with a decision to change. Most live up to that commitment. They correct the problem and maintain fully acceptable performance.

A few people fail to make the changes required to maintain membership in the organization. In these cases, termination is appropriate.

Is discharge punitive? A frequent misunderstanding involves the belief that while the Discipline Without Punishment system seems to have abolished minor forms of punishment (warnings, reprimands, unpaid suspensions), it retains the most severe form of punishment.

This misunderstanding results from the traditional progressive-discipline system's notion that termination is the final step of the discipline system: verbal reprimand, written warning, suspension without pay, discharge. This is a fallacy. Discharge is not the final step of the discipline system. Discharge is the failure of the discipline system.

The purpose of any discipline system, whether a traditional punitive approach or a nonpunitive procedure, is to convince the individual to stop his unacceptable behaviors and return to a fully acceptable level of performance. While the underlying philosophy and beliefs of the two systems are markedly different and the steps and tactics are entirely dissimilar, the goals of the two are the same. The error in the traditional approach is that it shows discharge as a final step. Traditional procedures miss the critical distinction that discharge is management's response only when all earlier efforts have failed to produce a satisfactory change. Now the organization finally concludes that its interests are best served if the employee is no longer a member of the team.

When a person returns from Decision Making Leave and continues to perform at an unacceptable level, there is no evidence that any further action will bring him to his senses and convince him to fly right. At this point we decide to terminate his employment. We terminate the employee not because we want to punish him, but because there is nothing else we can do that has any predictable chance of succeeding. Everything we have done to convince the individual to take responsibility for his behavior, correct that behavior, and return to acceptable norms has failed.

Even when we terminate for a first offense, the purpose is not punishment. While termination, referred to by arbitrators as the "capital punishment of organizational life," is certainly unpleasant, our intention is not retribution or to "pay him back" for what he has done. In these first-offense cases, usually involving issues of theft or assault or other outrageous behavior, we choose to terminate the offender because by committing that one intolerable act he has forfeited the right to the benefit of corrective action. By committing an act of theft, or assaulting a fellow employee, or selling drugs on the premises, he has demonstrated so little self-esteem and ability to conform to the minimum demands of a civilized society that his presence can no longer be tolerated.

Reaching the Termination Decision

The easiest firings are those produced by unexpected crises. Unprovoked, one employee hauls off and belts another. Your purchasing agent is revealed to be taking money on the sly. Two young summer interns are discovered, *in flagrante*, on the boardroom table.

These are easy because, regardless of whether any steps of the Discipline Without Punishment system have been taken, the provocation is clear and the remedy is obvious.

But these easy cases are rare. More difficult are those where the employee returns from a Decision Making Leave and subsequently commits an offense that would provoke a coaching session or an Oral Reminder if committed by an employee with an unblemished record. The most difficult arise when an individual is placed on a Decision Making Leave because his performance is simply not up to par. After his return he struggles to do the job right, but in spite of his sincere efforts his performance still is unacceptable and no compatible job exists within the organization.

Whatever scenario produces the decision to terminate, the manager's first responsibility is to the enterprise itself. Arrange the termination so that it occurs with the least damage to the company and fellow workers.

Creating a Plan

Start by creating a transition plan.

Good plans have three parts. The first part covers all the things you need to do before meeting with the individual to announce the termination. The second part involves the actual eyeball-to-eyeball meeting with the terminatee. This is your script—the exact words you will say to open the meeting, the checklist of points you will cover while the two of you are face-to-face. The third and final part of your plan covers exactly what will happen once the two of you shake hands and part company forever.

No organization allows managers to make the termination decision unilaterally. In every case the decision must be weighed and approved by senior officers in the line organization and the personnel function. Often the president is involved.

In creating the transition plan, choose the day and the time for the termination deliberately. While experts disagree on when a firing should occur, all acknowledge the importance of having a rationale, a good business reason for your choice of time and day for dropping the ax. Doing it early in the day, early in the week, encourages the employee to get right to work on finding another job and reduces the chances that he'll spend the weekend moping in a black hole or, worse, plotting revenge. Friday afternoons, on the other hand, often create the minimum amount of disruption to the rest of the staff.

Whatever your decision, put company interests first. For months you have probably put up with less than stellar performance in hopes that the situation would somehow correct itself. Now that the end is at hand, plan the transition to do the least damage to company and co-workers. You may want to start recruiting and wait until you've got a replacement ready to go before terminating. It may be in your best interests to send some subtle signals to clients and customers that there will be a staffing change soon.

If security is an issue, be prepared to escort the employee off the premises as soon as the termination has been announced. In industries like banking or computer software, where sabotage is a risk, restricting entry may be an unpleasant but necessary precaution. Every manager has heard horror stories of employees who left behind chaos by spitting gum in the works on their way out. A computer programmer, terminated by an encyclopedia publisher, got his final revenge after learning of his dismissal by reconfiguring the system to print the word *Allah* every time *Jesus* was to appear.

Run It by a Jury First

A good way to make sure that you are on solid ground in terminating an employee is to imagine yourself defending your action in front of a jury. Assume that you are on the witness stand and the employee's lawyer is attempting to prove that the firing was unjust, unfair, and vindictive.

Consider the questions the lawyer is likely to ask. The appropriate use of the Discipline Without Punishment system will convincingly answer all of the standard questions raised by a plaintiff's attorney:

Was the employee aware that his performance was unacceptable?
How do you know that he knew?
How often did you talk about it?
Have there been any disciplinary discussions? Do you have any documentation?
Was he given time to improve?
Was adequate training provided? Can you prove it?
Is there any information in the original employment application and other hiring data to suggest that poor placement is the real problem?

Look for anything that a third party could twist to suggest that the real reason for the termination is not the individual's performance but rather a personal grudge: Isn't that the real reason why you fired poor Smedley on his birthday, on the day before his tenth anniversary with the company, on the day before his pension vested, on the day his wife went into the hospital, on the day before his vacation started, on the day his mom died?

Don't fail to check any performance evaluations. Is there a record of unacceptable appraisals that confirm the disciplinary transactions? What do the last three evaluations actually say? Many times managers sugarcoat their appraisal ratings to avoid a confrontation, only to discover later on that the employee whose employment they want to terminate appears to be a model worker who possesses no major flaws.

Finally, are there any mitigating circumstances? Could a jury of his peers, neutral and unbiased, come to the conclusion that you acted outrageously?

In spite of all the publicity regarding wrongful termination cases, few employees ever take their former boss to court. The best way to keep out of court is to put yourself in the shoes of the employee's attorney, an EEOC investigator, or some other skeptical third party, and ask yourself how you would go about arguing that the employee was fired for some reason other than poor performance, unacceptable attendance, or inappropriate conduct.

Using "Peer Review" to Ensure Defensibility

A growing number of organizations are actually providing in-house juries just to make sure that all terminations result only for good business reasons. The most effective is a "Peer Review" system, where a terminated employee's case is heard by a panel of three fellow employees and two company managers. They ask the employee to state his case and then interview the supervisor, the personnel manager, and anyone else with relevant information. They check policies and precedents and then, through a secret majority-rules ballot, make a final and binding decision to uphold or reverse the termination.

Companies with this system encourage every terminated employee to grieve their discharge to the Peer Review panel. If the panel votes to overturn the decision and return the employee to work, the chances are good that a jury would have done the same. But if the panel votes to uphold the termination, as the great majority do, the employee is unlikely to protest further. Having agreed that the decision would be "final and binding" on both him and the company, he has had his day in court.

While many companies are initially nervous about giving a panel whose majority is made up of the employee's peers the power to reverse a termination decision, closer investigation reveals enormous benefits. Setting up a "due process" internal dispute resolution procedure is a powerful union-avoidance technique, since an impartial grievance procedure is about the only remaining benefit a union organizer can promise and actually deliver. Allowing employees to question policy decisions other than terminations ensures greater compliance with personnel policies. It encourages supervisors to make better decisions and to solve problems as soon as they arise.

Peer Review's biggest benefit may be its ability to keep problems out of court. A discharged employee whose protest has been heard and rejected by his peers is less likely to call a lawyer. If an employee does seek legal redress after his peers turn him down, his chances of prevailing are slim. Several recent court cases have upheld companies' ability to require employees to use their internal dispute resolution procedures before being allowed to turn to the outside. Other cases suggest that if the employee agrees that the panel's decision will be final and binding (as is the usual provision in Peer Review systems), he may be precluded from pursuing his case through the court system.

Companies with Peer Review procedures report that courts, civil rights commissions, state departments of labor, and other third parties regularly send cases back to use the company's internal grievance procedure. Employees serving on peer panels consistently demonstrate that they are as concerned with making good decisions as managers are. With recent legislation encouraging the use of alternative dispute resolution systems, interest in installing Peer Review as a way of keeping termination disputes out of court is flourishing.

Preparing a Script

Bungled terminations usually result from the manager's acting without thinking. Before you utter a word, write down the most important things you plan to say and then stick to your script.

Start by recognizing what you're up to. This is not a counseling session or a discussion about poor performance or another Discipline Without Punishment step. It is the announcement of an irrevocable decision to discharge the individual.

1. *Get right to the point.* Skip the small talk. Don't put off the inevitable. All of your attempts to put the person at ease will backfire if you don't get immediately to the job at hand. Start by saying, "Hello, John. Thank you for coming in. I've got some bad news for you." By announcing right from the start that there is bad news ahead, you will rivet the individual's attention on what's coming next.

2. *Break the bad news.* State the reason for the termination in one or two short sentences and then tell the person directly that he has been terminated: "As you know, John, we have talked several times about the quality problems in your area. You have been through all the steps of our Discipline Without Punishment procedure. But last month's report indicated that your unit still has the lowest quality index. We have decided that a change must be made, and as of today your employment has been terminated."

Or, "Sally, we've talked before about your failure to respond promptly to customer inquiries and complaints. When you returned from your Decision Making Leave you told me that you would correct the problem, but since then I have had two more complaints from customers. After these last complaints I realized that the situation is not working out. I have decided that a change must be made and that today will be your last day with us."

Or, "Walt, when your forklift hit the wall yesterday, I told you that this was a very serious safety problem. I said then that I would need to get all of the information and get back to you to let you know what we would do. I have now completed my investigation of the accident. Because of the seriousness of this incident, we have decided to terminate your employment with the company."

In each case, the manager is focusing on the problem or the performance, not on the person. There is no need to be brutal. John or Sally or Walt is still an honorable and worthwhile human being. He or she is simply no longer an employee of your company.

In the course of writing down exactly what you will say to break the bad news, ask yourself the question, What do I know for sure? The answer to that question will help you decide how to phrase your announcement. For example, you don't know for sure that John is unconcerned with quality. You do know that he is the section supervisor and that his section has the lowest quality index of any. You don't know for sure that Sally doesn't care about handling customer complaints quickly. You do know that you recently received two more letters from customers objecting to the way their complaints were handled. And you don't know for sure that Walt is a reckless driver; you do know that he ran his forklift into the wall.

Note that in each of these cases the manager directly announces that the employee has been terminated. The individual is being told of something that has already happened, not advised of something that will happen in the future. It is easier to focus the individual's attention on the fact that his future lies elsewhere if he clearly hears the statement that the decision has been made, the door has been shut. The decision cannot be revoked or reversed. The ball game is over.

3. *Listen to what the employee has to say.* There are several predictable reactions to the news that one has just lost his job. The most common are shock, denial, anger, and grief. Listening to what the employee says will tell you which of the reactions he is experiencing. Your response will be more effective if you know how he is taking the news.

Listening carefully will also tell you whether the employee has accepted the reality that he is no longer a member of the organization. You can't move forward to talk about what will happen from here until he accepts the fact that his employment is through.

Listening also demonstrates compassion. When people complain to the EEOC, a state human rights commission, or other third party, their initial complaint frequently involves not their belief that they were discriminated against but their feeling that they weren't treated fairly. Treating someone unfairly, while deplorable, is probably not illegal. Treating someone fairly—giving her a chance to explain; listening to what he has to say—can often eliminate the individual's desire to complain about mistreatment to an official outsider.

When you listen to the now former employee's response to the news that he no longer works for you, avoid the tendency to be a counselor. Don't argue about whether a good decision has been made. For better or worse, the die has been cast and it is in the best interests of both parties to move on to brighter tomorrows.

How is the employee taking the news? If the reaction is shock, don't try to prove to the person that he should have seen it coming. Instead, acknowledge the emotion and make sure that the message gets across.

Anger is the reaction that managers fear the most: "You can't do this to me! I'll show you! I'll get you for this!" We've been spooked by so many "Unhappy Worker Guns Down Boss" headlines that we morbidly anticipate its possibility anytime we lower the boom. Fortunately, anger is the least common response. Anger can be diffused by listening and avoiding any debate about the merits of the action. Be firm, repeat the decision, and let the employee vent his feelings. Then say, "I can see that you're angry, Paul. It's an understandable reaction. What you need to do, though, is channel your energy into thinking about what you're going to do next."

Denial may be the most difficult reaction to deal with. There have been several cases where an employee who had been told that he had been fired went right back to his desk and picked up where he had left off before the meeting, explaining that there were several projects he had to finish before he could leave. When "I can't believe that this is happening" is the employee's response, your job is to make sure he gets the message. Repeat, restate, and talk about what the next steps will be.

In a classic case, a cowardly manager tried to dismiss an employee by leaving the pink slip in his top desk drawer, where he was sure to see it when he returned from vacation. The employee opened the drawer, saw the note, and went into instant denial. He threw the pink slip away and started to work, pretending he never got it. The manager was afraid to confront him about it, the employee improved his performance to a minimally tolerable level. Neither ever spoke of the incident again.

Grief is almost always present, and no manager should begin a termination discussion without a box of tissues at arm's reach. When the need arises, take the box, offer a tissue, wait until the employee has regained his composure somewhat, and keep the discussion moving.

Whatever the reaction, listening to the employee will increase the odds that he will accept the unhappy decision maturely and concentrate his attention on moving to the next stage of his career. Nodding silently while the employee is speaking, making the sounds that indicate that you're paying attention ("uh-huh," "I see," "ummmmm," etc.), and pausing after you ask a question will demonstrate that you've heard the person out.

Keep It Short

Once you have written your script for the meeting, it is wise to prepare a written termination summary that spells out all of the information the person needs to know. The termination summary will answer questions like these:

How long will I continue to be paid?
What will happen to my health insurance? My life insurance? My retirement plan or 401k?
What support can I expect in looking for a new job: access to an office? a phone? outplacement assistance?
What will be said when people call about a reference?

Putting a written termination statement in the individual's hand helps the manager communicate that the decision is irrevocable. It also demonstrates the organization's belief that the interests of both parties are best served if there is a clear statement that summarizes all of the issues that surround the termination. Finally, the termination statement helps keep the meeting short.

At this point there's not much to talk about. The time for coaching and problem solving has passed. Once the employee has accepted the reality of the termination, reviewing the details of the termination statement is the first step toward beginning a new life in a different place.

If the person still hasn't fully accepted the finality of the situation, explain how you will present the termination to people inside the company and then ask, "How do you plan to break the news to your family and friends?"

Bring the meeting to a close by specifically explaining the next step. When the employee asks, "What do I do now?" you should be able to answer that question in detail. If you are fortunate enough to have the services of an outplacement counselor, the answer is to take the person to the room where the counselor is waiting, introduce the two of them, and let the professional take over. If you're doing it on your own, decide whether the employee can go back to his work area or must exit company premises immediately. If she can return to the work area, will it be to finish the rest of the day or just to clear personal belongings out of her desk? If he is leaving directly, how will he get his stuff?

If you're doing it without outside help, it's usually best to schedule the termination meeting at the end of a workday so that the meeting takes place while co-workers are leaving. After the meeting (ten minutes is sufficient, more than twenty is excessive) walk with the employee back to his desk and wait while he collects any personal items. Anything too big can be put in one corner for later pickup or delivery; the rest can be taken directly. Walk to the exit together, shake hands, wish him well, and part with both of your dignities intact.

Avoiding Misdirected Compassion

One final note. Twenty-five years of watching the management scene has convinced me that the biggest problem with terminations is that they don't happen often enough.

Most managers are compassionate people, but when the need arises to terminate a subordinate their compassion is often misdirected. They become so concerned about the adverse impact on the employee to be discharged that they forget about all the people who manage to do their jobs and meet the manager's expectations in spite of having as many personal problems and difficulties as the terminatee has.

While managers are appropriately concerned with how one person's termination will affect the rest of the work group, usually they discover that co-workers are singing, "Thank God and Greyhound She's Gone." His peers are the ones who have had to work harder to make up for his shortcomings and sloughings-off. When terminations are well justified and professionally executed, the rest of the work group realizes that the discipline system actually works. If the termination is handled with dignity and grace, the notion that this is a good place to work is strengthened.

But when obvious losers and shirkers and occupational ne'er-do-wells are allowed to continue in their positions unchallenged, the message to the talented and energetic is that this is a place to avoid. Those who can find other jobs leave; the ones who stay are those who prefer an employer with low standards.

9

The Administration of the Discipline System

Besides the inherent flaws of the traditional, punitive progressive-discipline system, there is another problem that causes this procedure to be an ineffective problem-solving tool: the way in which the system is administered.

Supervisors often hesitate to initiate a step of disciplinary action. Besides their reluctance to be punitive, a more subtle reason causes them to pause: They don't know the answers to many of the questions that arise when the discipline procedure is begun:

> Whose permission do I have to get before I can hold a disciplinary transaction?
> Exactly how is it supposed to be documented?
> Who gets copies of the documentation?
> Should I ask the employee to sign a copy?
> How long does it stay in effect? What do I say if the employee requests a transfer?
> What if she says she wants to appeal?

Whatever system an organization uses, these administrative issues must be resolved for supervisors to feel confident that they are taking appropriate action. More important, these issues must be resolved if the management of the enterprise is going to feel confident that disciplinary discussions are being held appropriately, consistently, and within the guidelines of company policy.

In this chapter I will identify and address every major administrative issue that must be resolved for any system of disciplinary action to work. I will review the alternatives available, the benefits and limitations of each, and the decisions that organizations that have implemented the Discipline Without Punishment system have made. Even for organizations that plan no change to the formal steps of their current approach, a review and updating of their current administrative procedures can greatly increase the effectiveness of the system.

As illustrated in Figure 9-1, the complete Discipline Without Punishment system has a total of six individual elements, including the three formal levels of disciplinary action.

Some administrative questions or issues may not apply directly to every element. For example, "Maximum number allowed?" is irrelevant when termination is the element under consideration; "Appealable through the Grievance Procedure?" is rarely a concern with regard to Positive Contacts. Still it is helpful to make sure that all administrative aspects are considered for each element of the system.

Figure 9-1. The elements of the Discipline Without Punishment system.

INFORMAL TRANSACTIONS

Positive Contact
Coaching Session

FORMAL DISCIPLINARY TRANSACTIONS

Level 1 Oral Reminder
Level 2 Written Reminder
Level 3 Decision Making Leave

TERMINATION

Termination

The Elements of Administration

Initiator

Who should be the person responsible for initiating the action in question?

Almost without exception, every organization feels that the immediate supervisor (at whatever level) is the person who bears the responsibility for initiating each element of Discipline Without Punishment. Making anyone other than the direct supervisor responsible for initiating action reduces supervisory authority. By holding the immediate supervisor responsible the organization reinforces the importance of the first-line supervisor's job.

In some companies it is not always clear who an individual's immediate supervisor is, particularly when matrix structures or self-directed work teams or working foremen (nonmanagement employees who provide work direction and handle administrative details) are used. In an implementation of Discipline Without Punishment in a large hospital, one difficult issue involved determining the responsibility of "charge nurses" for handling disciplinary action.

One way to resolve the issue is to determine who would be responsible for giving the individual a performance appraisal and salary increase. That same person is probably the most appropriate candidate to handle any disciplinary transactions required.

Prior Approval

Whose approval is regarded before the planned action can be taken?

No organization requires the immediate supervisor to gain anyone else's approval before conducting a positive contact or coaching session. These are considered regular, ongoing elements of any supervisor's job.

Some organizations allow supervisors to conduct an Oral Reminder discussion without the prior approval of anyone else in the organization. Other companies, particularly those whose supervisors have not had much experience or formal management training, require them to get approval from their immediate supervisor or department head before holding the discussion. Few require the personnel department to be involved at the Oral Reminder level.

Almost all organizations require the immediate supervisor to get approval from both the department head and human resources before conducting a Written Reminder discussion.

At the Decision Making Leave and termination steps, most organizations require that these actions be approved in advance by the department head, a senior human resources manager, and a member of senior management.

Witness Required?

Is a management witness required to be present during the conversation with the employee?

No organization requires a management witness to be present for coaching sessions or Positive Contact discussions. Few require a witness in order for the supervisor to conduct an Oral Reminder transaction. Many require a witness at the Written Reminder stage, and almost all organizations require a management witness to be present when an employee is placed on a Decision Making Leave or terminated.

In every case where a witness is present, however, the organization expects the immediate supervisor to be the initiator of the transaction and to conduct the discussion. The witness's role is simply to be a witness.

In unionized organizations, the employee's union representative must be present at the time any disciplinary discussion is conducted, or at the time that the employee is involved in the investigation of a situation that could possibly lead to disciplinary action. Few nonunion organizations allow employees to bring a witness or representative to the meeting, except in the rare cases where language differences require a translator.

Documentation

How will the action be formally documented once it has been taken?

The documentation procedures for coaching sessions and the three formal steps of the Discipline Without Punishment system are covered in full in the chapters on those steps. Positive Contacts are typically documented with an informal note to the employee or, if the employee's action was particularly meritorious, with a formal memo to the individual with copies to senior management.

Terminations can be documented with a summary memo to the file with a complete chronological listing of all the events that led up to the termination. All documents relating to previous disciplinary action should be collected and filed with this summary memo.

Distribution

Who gets copies of the documentation? Where will the records be held?

Records of Positive Contacts, coaching sessions, and Oral Reminders are usually kept in the departmental file, not in the employee's permanent personnel record. Many attorneys, however, advise that there should only be one real personnel file and encourage organizations not to maintain any form of personnel records with the department.

For Written Reminders and Decision Making Leaves, the original of the memo documenting the discussion goes to the employee; the supervisor who wrote the memo retains a copy. Other copies of the memo are sent to the department head and the personnel department for inclusion in the employee's official records. Additional copies of the memo, particularly at the Decision Making Leave step, may be sent to other senior managers, particularly if they were involved in approving that action. All documentation regarding termination is kept with the rest of the former employee's records.

Length of Time Active

If the employee improves his performance, corrects the problem, and maintains satisfactory performance for a significant period of time, should he have the right to have his slate wiped clean?

Most organizations agree that allowing the employee to get disciplinary action deactivated after the problem has been corrected is a good idea, particularly since the chance to purge one's file of detrimental information is a significant incentive for improvement. Few, however, have developed workable procedures for "deactivating" disciplinary action.

In the course of implementing Discipline Without Punishment, organizations begin by first coming to agreement that they will establish a formal mechanism for deactivating disciplinary action. They then must decide how long each step will stay in effect. Most decide that the time frames should vary, with initial steps being deactivated quickly and later steps remaining active for a longer period of time.

The following matrix reflects the range of decisions that companies that have implemented Discipline Without Punishment have made regarding the length of time a step will remain active:

ACTIVE DURATION OF DISCIPLINE WITHOUT PUNISHMENT STEPS

Step	Shortest Time Period	Longest Time Period
Oral Reminder	3 months	12 months
Written Reminder	6 months	18 months
Decision Making Leave	9 months	24 months

Most organizations decide to deactivate the disciplinary action in the same way that it was activated. In other words, if the Written Reminder step was formally documented with a memo to the employee with copies to the department head and the personnel file, it seems reasonable to deactivate the action with a similar memo with copies distributed to the same recipients. The memo should recognize the individual for correcting the problem and maintaining the improvement over a significant period of time.

There may be exceptional situations where unique conditions require special provisions. For example, an airline that was implementing the Discipline Without Punishment system encountered a major obstacle when the time frames for deactivation were being determined. While all of the managers involved in the implementation were comfortable with a recommendation that Written Reminders would remain active for six months and Decision Making Leaves for one full year, the vice president of flight operations was adamant that any disciplinary offense committed by a pilot that affected operational safety remain active forever. They ended up adopting a policy that provided for the six month/twelve month time frame, supplemented by a footnote that specified that any issues that dealt specifically with flight safety would be decided on an ad hoc basis.

What should be done with the memo documenting the disciplinary action that was placed in the individual's personnel file? Most companies remove it from the person's file and place it in a separate "Dead Disciplinary Action" file on a chronological or alphabetical basis. In this way the employee's future prospects will not be compromised long after a problem has been resolved by retaining an antiquated disciplinary notice in the personnel file, yet the record will still be available if needed to demonstrate organizational consistency in actions taken with others.

When Can Steps Be Repeated?

How many Oral Reminders or Written Reminders may a person receive before moving to the next more serious level?

Every organization agrees that a person may receive an unlimited number of Positive Contacts and coaching sessions.

Almost all allow an employee to receive more than one Oral Reminder. The caveat, however, is that they must be given for unrelated problems.

As described earlier, all disciplinary problems fall neatly into one of three mutually exclusive categories: attendance, performance, and conduct. Most organizations with Discipline Without Punishment allow an individual to receive two or even three Oral Reminders, provided that they result from problems in different categories. Thus a person who received an Oral Reminder for excessive absenteeism (an issue in the attendance category) might receive a second Oral Reminder for failing to meet a deadline (a performance issue, unrelated to attendance). However, the same individual would usually be given a Written Reminder if a problem of tardiness arose after the initial Oral Reminder for excessive absences. While tardiness was not exactly the same offense, it falls into the same category, attendance.

Organizations often decide to allow a person to receive more than one Written Reminder, again provided that the problems triggering the action are in different categories. However, every organization considers the Decision Making Leave to be a singular event. Since the employee is required to make a commitment to totally acceptable performance in every area of his job, there is little justification for allowing the step to be repeated.

And terminations? Only one per customer, please.

When Can Steps Be Skipped?

When an individual commits a serious disciplinary infraction, can early steps be skipped and a Written Reminder or Decision Making Leave step be taken directly? What are the situations that justify termination for a first offense?

Throughout this book the assumption has been that when employee problems arise, they arise at a level of seriousness low enough to allow the manager to seek a solution through training or job engineering interventions. If these initial approaches do not work, then the manager proceeds, in order, through holding a coaching session and then the steps of the Discipline Without Punishment procedure. While this assumption is valid for the majority of problems that arise, there are offenses so serious that training or coaching or even an Oral Reminder is inappropriate. And there are rare cases where termination is appropriate even for a first offense.

The most manageable way to separate the lower-level offenses from the more serious ones is to assign all disciplinary problems into one of three categories: minor, serious, and major.

Minor problems, the great majority, are those that do not involve issues of honesty or trust, do not by themselves constitute a threat to the operation of the business, and pose no threat to the safety or well-being of the individual or other employees. Excessive tardiness, poor housekeeping, overstaying breaks, and other minor inefficiencies are examples of problems at this level of seriousness. For these problems, if training and coaching are not sufficient to bring about a change, the discipline process would begin with the Oral Reminder and continue through the remaining steps.

Serious problems are those which do constitute a threat to the operation of the business or to the safety of the employee or other individuals. These may include violations like smoking in a room where oxygen is in use, gambling on company property, showing up for to work in unfit condition, reporting a false reason for an absence, or being absent without notification. For these offenses, either a Written Reminder or a Decision Making Leave would be considered appropriate by most companies. The final decision would depend on the actual seriousness of the violation, the employee's work record, the action the company had previously taken in similar cases, and the supervisor's best judgment about which step would be the more effective in solving the problem.

Finally, there are major violations. These are acts which threaten the operation of the business or the safety of individuals, or demonstrate, in and of themselves, that the offender has so little personal integrity and self-esteem that his continued presence cannot be tolerated. Deliberate falsification of records, theft and fraud, assaulting a supervisor or co-worker or customer, selling drugs on the premises, and possession of firearms are almost always considered major offenses.

Discharge is the appropriate remedy for major offenses. However, it is important that the employee never be discharged at the time of the incident. If the employee is terminated in the heat of the moment, he is almost sure to be returned to work if the termination is later challenged. The arbitrator or hearing officer or judge will determine that in spite of the employee's actions, the company responded without conducting any investigation or letting cooler heads prevail.

Use the statement "You are suspended pending investigation" at the time of the incident and remove the individual from the premises. Once the employee has left (and it may be necessary to call security or the police), the company can make a full investigation and determine if there are any mitigating circumstances that would preclude the decision to terminate. Even when the violation is flagrant and the facts are clear, it is only to the organization's benefit to wait until the following day to make the termination decision official. In this way, if the action is ever challenged later, the company can testify truthfully that at the time of the incident the individual was not terminated but was suspended. After sleeping on it overnight and seeking in vain for any mitigating circumstance, the company made a sober and objective decision to terminate.

This suspension is not a part of the formal discipline process. It is an emergency action taken to allow the organization the time required to determine which element of the Discipline Without Punishment system is appropriate. The time the employee spends away from work on a crisis suspension is normally without pay, unless the investigation concludes that the suspension was unjustified.

In short: There is no offense that an employee can commit that justifies termination on the spot.

Is the Action Appealable?

Can the individual appeal the action through an existing internal dispute resolution procedure (e.g., open-door policy, Peer Review procedure, grievance system)?

Employees who are represented by a union will automatically have access to a formal grievance procedure that provides for the complaint ultimately to be heard and resolved by an outside arbitrator. Nonunion organizations that have open-door policies typically allow employees who feel that disciplinary action or discharge actions were inappropriate to appeal them to the president or other senior officer. While few open-door policies provide any genuine due-process protections for the employee, they may suggest some semblance of organizational fairness. Many are adopting Peer Review systems to allow final and binding internal resolution of employment disputes.

While appeal procedures are inappropriate for Positive Contacts or coaching sessions, most companies allow employees to use any available appeal mechanisms for any step of the discipline process. In addition, companies that have created Peer Review or other internal due-process dispute resolution systems actively encourage all terminated employees to file a grievance. Most of the time the decision to terminate is upheld and the individual, having had his day in court, is less likely to pursue legal action. On the other hand, if the peer panel decides to reinstate the terminated employee, the odds are great that a jury or hearing officer would have come to the same conclusion. As a result, the company can save a great deal of money in back pay and punitive damages, as well as avoid negative publicity, by establishing and encouraging the use of a final and binding internal grievance mechanism.

Eligible for Transfer?

If the company has a procedure whereby employees can request transfer, promotion, or upgrade from the jobs they currently hold, is an individual allowed to request transfer while he is on an active step of disciplinary action?

If the company allows individuals to apply for a transfer to a different department, or to request an upgrade or promotion, one of the implementation tasks is to decide whether someone who is on an active step of discipline will be allowed to use this procedure.

Reactions of organizations vary. Some companies prohibit the use of the transfer request until an employee successfully completes the active period of any disciplinary step, believing that a person should correct his problem and be at a minimally acceptable level of performance before being allowed to request a transfer to a different department. Others allow an employee on an Oral Remainder to use the transfer request system but prohibit its use at more serious levels. Most prohibit employee-initiated transfers during the active period of a Decision Making Leave.

This of course does not apply to any company-initiated transfer or promotion. The organization can always decide to transfer or promote an individual, even though that person may be on an active step of the Discipline Without Punishment procedure.

If an employee is allowed to transfer, however, this never affects the active period of the disciplinary action.

Eligible for Compensation Change?

If the individual becomes eligible for a compensation change while on an active step of the discipline procedure (e.g., cost-of-living increase, annual salary adjustment, merit increase), will the increase be granted or will it be deferred/delayed/denied until the action is no longer active?

If an automatic, across-the-board compensation change is

granted to all organization members, there is little justification to withholding this change from those individuals who are currently on an active step of disciplinary action. The only criterion for receiving this type of salary or wage adjustment is simply being on the company's payroll.

But if an employee becomes eligible for a merit increase or other individually determined compensation adjustment while he is on an active step of disciplinary action, should the increase be granted? Several possibilities exist:

1. Grant the increase and take no account of the fact that the individual is on an active step of discipline.
2. Grant the increase but reduce the amount to reflect the seriousness of the disciplinary action.
3. Delay the increase until the disciplinary action becomes inactive, then grant the full amount of the increase retroactive to the date on which the employee became eligible.
4. Delay the increase until the disciplinary action becomes inactive, then grant the increase effective on the date when the disciplinary action became deactivated.

Of these four possibilities, the one that is probably the easiest to manage and to justify to the individual is the fourth. Most organizations feel that it makes little sense to take a step which places an individual in jeopardy of ultimately losing his job and then turn around and send an entirely contradictory message by awarding that person a "merit" increase.

Discipline During the "Probationary Period"

Most organizations decide that the formal Discipline Without Punishment system will not apply during the employee's initial employment or "probationary" period. They believe that access to the discipline system is an employee benefit which the employee earns by demonstrating sufficient self-discipline to become a member of the regular workforce.

It is reasonable for a manager to assume that the performance, behavior, and demeanor that he sees during the initial employment

Figure 9-2.   Sample policy matrix for Discipline Without Punishment.

ACTION Issue	Initiator	Prior Approval	Documentation	Employee Signature Required?	Witness Required?	Distribution	Length of Time Active	Maximum Number Allowed	Appealable?	Eligible for Transfer?	Eligible Comp. Change?
INFORMAL DISCUSSIONS											
POSITIVE CONTACT	Immediate Supervisor	None	Informal note (optional)	N/A	No	N/A	N/A	N/A	N/A	Yes	Yes
COACHING SESSION	Immediate Supervisor	None	Performance Discussion Worksheet (Optional)	No	No	Department File	N/A	N/A	N/A	Yes	Yes
FORMAL DISCIPLINE LEVELS											
ORAL REMINDER	Immediate Supervisor	Dept. Head	Perf. Disc. Worksheet	No	Optional	Department File	3 mos.	3	Yes	Yes	Yes
WRITTEN REMINDER	Immediate Supervisor	Dept. Head and HR	PDW and Memo to Emp.	No	Yes	Original - Emp. Copies - HR & Dept. File	6 mos.	2	Yes	Yes	No
DECISION MAKING LEAVE	Immediate Supervisor	Dept. Head and HR	PDW and Memo to Emp.	Yes	Yes	Original - Emp. Copies - HR & Dept. File	12 mos.	1	Yes	No	No
TERMINATION											
TERMINATION	Immediate Supervisor	Dept. Head and HR	Chronological Summary	N/A	Yes	Human Resources	N/A	N/A	Yes	N/A	N/A

period are the finest that the employee is capable of. If a performance problem arises with a new employee that would be serious enough to warrant a coaching session with a regular employee, the manager should hold a very serious discussion with the individual and consider whether the new employee is properly suited for this job at this company. If the problem continues, or if a problem serious enough to warrant a formal disciplinary conversation arises at any time during the initial employment period, the most appropriate response is termination.

The Policy Matrix

In the course of resolving the basic policy and procedural issues involved in an implementation of the Discipline Without Punishment system, many companies create a "policy matrix." This document provides on a single page complete administrative guidelines and is of immense value to supervisors.

In Figure 9-2 you will find an actual matrix created by one organization as part of its implementation of Discipline Without Punishment. While the decisions represented on this matrix would not be appropriate for all organizations, they are reasonable and appropriate for their culture, history, and organizational mission.

10

Creating a Discipline Without Punishment System

Individual managers can achieve a great deal of personal success by applying the techniques of dealing with people in a nonpunitive way. However, an organization-wide implementation of Discipline Without Punishment requires a major cultural change effort. Formal policies and informal day-to-day practices must be reviewed and reconsidered. Supervisors need to be trained in the new approach, the belief system behind it, and the techniques for holding nonpunitive disciplinary discussions. They must learn how to develop action plans that lead to an employee's agreement to change and recommit to the company's objectives. Management must communicate to everyone concerned the general purpose of the system, the specific administrative practices, and the commitment of senior executives to this new way of life.

Management must also link the system with all other existing human resources policies and programs: performance appraisal, attendance management, grievance and appeal mechanisms, employee-assistance programs. The training provided managers must be synchronized with other training and management development efforts so that all development efforts are seen as integral parts of an overall strategy and not as merely another "program of the month." Finally, after installing the new program, managers must measure, monitor, and maintain it.

The implementation process typically involves several months of work: analyzing alternatives, reviewing the experience of other

organizations, making decisions, training managers, building organization-wide understanding and acceptance. To be fully effective
and widely supported, it will require the efforts of a large number
of managers and supervisors, both from the various line departments and human resources professionals. These efforts will produce a unique policy statement that addresses all issues and reflects
the specific culture and values of the organization, as well as a cadre
of managers who understand it thoroughly, support it fully, and
use it well.

Twenty years of work with some of the best-managed organizations in the United States to help them install the Discipline Without
Punishment system has resulted in the development of a straightforward and consistent implementation process that any company can
follow. In this chapter I will describe the implementation procedure
as it would apply to a large organization with several organizational
units and a large number of employees, perhaps a thousand or so.
As long as appropriate modifications are made, the same approach
can be used in much smaller organizations to effect a successful implementation of Discipline Without Punishment. Large or small,
three critical components determine the success of a Discipline
Without Punishment implementation: the development of suitable
policies and procedures, the training of all managers, and the cre-
ation of organization-wide understanding, support, and acceptance.

Where to Begin

The decision to implement a Discipline Without Punishment system
usually begins when one individual in the organization becomes
aware that there is an alternative to traditional ways of handling disciplinary problems. Implementation begins with illumination—a
light dawns in the mind of one person, whether a line manager or a
member of the human resources function, that a better way exists.

From this point the idea of change must be sold within the organization. Since replacing the organization's current system for handling matters of discipline with the Discipline Without Punishment
approach is a matter of policy, the company's policy-making officials
must be involved in the decision.

While the agreement of senior management can be obtained

through meetings with individual executives and the building of support one-on-one, a more rapid and effective strategy is to conduct an "executive overview" of the approach for a group of key line and staff managers once the organization's curiosity has been tweaked. The purpose of this meeting is not to decide to implement Discipline Without Punishment; it is rather to give everyone concerned enough information to decide whether Discipline Without Punishment is an approach that is consistent with the values and culture of the organization. If the executive overview is approached more as an educational and exploratory opportunity than a marketing and decision-making session, the chances for favorable consideration rise.

The Executive Overview Agenda

Successful executive overviews share two common characteristics: They provide full information on the rationale and mechanics of the Discipline Without Punishment approach, and they demonstrate the need for the system based on the history and current conditions within the organization.

Information on the operation of Discipline Without Punishment can be obtained from this book as well as from the experience of other organizations that are using the approach successfully. Managers will want answers to such questions as:

What types of companies are using the approach?
Why is a nonpunitive system more appropriate for our company, our people, and our managers than what we are doing now?
What benefits are we likely to gain?
What administrative issues will need to be resolved?
How do the policies and practices of Discipline Without Punishment compare with what we're doing now?
What kind of implementation process will be required for our organization? How long will it take? Who needs to be involved?
How will we know that the new system is successful?

How much will it cost, both directly and indirectly, to implement Discipline Without Punishment?

Current data from inside the organization itself can be used to demonstrate the need for an approach that emphasizes commitment and personal responsibility and eliminates punishment. Begin by looking for data on how well the current system is working:

How many disciplinary incidents occurred in the last year?
How serious were these incidents—how many verbal reprimands, how many suspensions, etc.?
What kinds of problems caused disciplinary action to be taken?
How many people resolved the problem following a disciplinary conversation? How many moved on to the next step?
How many people were terminated? How many of these terminations were grieved or otherwise challenged?

While these data will be useful in demonstrating the need, few organizations have the monitoring and tracking systems in place that allow this information to be easily captured. Fortunately, problems with the existing system usually are not the major impetus for an organization's changing to a nonpunitive approach.

The primary reason that organizations make the change is not that their current system isn't working well. The reason is that, whether the system is working well or poorly, the underlying adversarial philosophy and punitive mentality do not fit with the values and vision of the organization as it is. The traditional discipline system is used by most organizations not because they embrace its values and assumptions about people, but because they know of no other.

There are actually few organizations that abandon their current practices and move to a nonpunitive approach because their existing system is provoking the same kind of hostility and resentment that prevailed in the Frito-Lay plant that caused the approach to be created. A far greater number of companies are moving because they have outgrown the assumptions that underlie the traditional approach. What they have done for years no longer fits.

More valuable data, therefore, may come from opinion and attitude surveys the organization has conducted. Do employees feel that they are being treated with dignity and respect? Do supervisors feel confident in confronting a lapse from organizational grace? Are senior managers confident that the way supervisors are handling disciplinary problems is shielding the organization from legal challenge? Does everyone agree that the discipline system treats people the way that they themselves would like to be treated if their behavior or performance ever warranted a disciplinary rejoinder?

Meetings with both managers and employees, either in one-on-one sessions or through focus groups, can help point out the need for change. When James City County, the county government for the Jamestown and Williamsburg region of Virginia, was considering the implementation of Discipline Without Punishment, senior personnel analyst Kelly Medlin held a series of focus group meetings with senior managers, first-line supervisors, and nonmanagement employees. She asked each group the same three questions:

1. Why do we need a discipline system?
2. What drives you crazy about our current system?
3. What do you love about our system?

The answers to these questions, she found, gave her a great store of data to use in getting back to the senior staff to demonstrate the need to consider implementing a different approach.

Three motivations typically propel an organization into accepting the need for change: proactive reasons, reactive reasons, and the need to increase overall effectiveness. Proactive reasons include the need to align the discipline system more closely with organizational values and the desire to provide more formal mechanisms to recognize the good performance on the part of the overwhelming majority of employees. Reactive reasons include the needs to reduce the number of disciplinary transactions, to reduce exposure to the risk of workplace violence, and to increase defensibility to legal or arbitration challenge, and the desire to solve morale problems resulting from unfair or inconsistent disciplinary action.

Finally, the desire to increase organizational effectiveness shows up in concerns about equipping supervisors to handle employee problems quickly and confidently, to make sure that performance management policies are thoroughly understood and consistently applied, and concerns about providing managers with the most effective tools to get the job done.

The executive overview is the ideal launching pad for the implementation of Discipline Without Punishment. At this session all of the questions and issues get raised and resolved. Equally important, a common foundation of understanding is created so that organization-wide support and acceptance is likely to follow.

Creating Organizational Ownership

When organizational change efforts fail, the primary reason is rarely a deficiency in the new system or program itself. Most of the time failure results from a lack of ownership.

Without ownership, almost anything will tarnish and corrode. A few years ago I accompanied a group of wonderfully talented junior high and high school musicians from the SMU Conservatory on a concert tour of the then Soviet Union. On the morning of our final performance, we entered the concert hall at the Moscow Conservatory where that night these bright precollege performers would play their final concert to an audience of their peers, the finest young musicians in Russia.

We walked onto the stage where a generation before, Van Cliburn, then only a few years older than these talented teenagers, had electrified the world by becoming the first American to win the Tchaikovsky competition. In the center of the stage stood a piano. The same one Van Cliburn had played that night? The one we recall from all of the pictures? I walked over to it.

It was filthy. While it was constantly in use, it had been years since it had been cleaned or waxed. It was covered with fingerprints and grease smears from the fingers of dirty hands practicing. Any part that was not regularly touched was covered with a thick layer of grime.

Astounded, I asked our guide/interpreter why the piano was in such terrible condition. She turned to an older woman nearby, a worker in the Moscow Conservatory, and asked her about it.

"That piano?" the old woman snorted. "That's Gorbachev's piano. Gorbachev owns that piano. . . . Let Gorbachev come here and clean it up!"

Without ownership, nobody cares.

To ensure success there must be shared ownership on the part of everyone who has a stake in the system's success. The best way to ensure the success of Discipline Without Punishment, as dozens of organizations have discovered, is to create an Implementation Team and charge them with the responsibility of tailoring the system and assuring a smooth transition from the organization's current practices to the Discipline Without Punishment approach. Among the tasks that the team must accomplish are these:

- Establish the degree of management authority at each level of the system.
- Clarify the specific roles and responsibilities of line management, human resources, and top management.
- Develop procedures for deactivating disciplinary action when an employee has successfully solved a problem.
- Determine the severity of various infractions.
- Develop effective documentation procedures.
- Identify any unique training needs.
- Link Discipline Without Punishment and all other related performance management programs.
- Develop organization-wide understanding and support.

This Implementation Team is a task force of ten to twenty individuals from different functions in the organization and different levels of management. Members are almost always management level employees, from first-line supervisors up to senior operating officers, including specialized individual contributors like a representative from the corporate counsel's office and human resources and training specialists.

While a few companies have successfully included nonmanagement employees on the Implementation Team, virtually none have invited union representatives to participate in the development of the system. In spite of the productive relationship that many companies enjoy with their union and their view that including the union president or business agent on the Implementation Team will enhance that relationship, I recommend against it.

Several years ago I was managing the implementation of Discipline Without Punishment with a large oil company in Houston. The company had worked for several years to develop a partnership relationship with the union and we all anticipated we could further that goal by including a shop steward and the local president on the team. Our plan worked reasonably well until the day that the Implementation Team was assessing the severity levels of different infractions—which offenses were minor, which were serious, which would be considered a major violation.

In the middle of the discussion, the union president called a recess and asked that he and the shop steward be excused from service on the Implementation Team. "We really can't participate in this," he explained. "If we agree that sleeping on the job is a major offense, then we've really compromised our ability to process a grievance for a member who might get terminated for sleeping. You guys need to make those decisions by yourself."

He was right, of course. The job of management is to make the rules; the union's responsibility is to make sure that management plays by the rules it has made. If those roles are compromised, then both sides suffer and the employee himself will surely be the loser.

A corollary is that in most cases management does have the right to implement the Discipline Without Punishment approach unilaterally without negotiations with the union. Several arbitrations have upheld the right of management to implement any discipline system it wanted, assuming it met reasonable tests of fair play and due process. Unions have the right to grieve any action taken under that system if it is inconsistent, excessive, or otherwise unfair. Only in situations where the specific steps of the traditional progressive-discipline system are codified in the union contract does management have to negotiate the change with the union, and this can usually be accomplished by a joint letter of agreement. Few unions have raised any genuine objection to the elimination of warnings and unpaid suspensions; most have accepted the change with a note of "skeptical acceptance." They find little to complain about in the theory but are suspicious about whether managers will actually walk their talk. Several unions in fact have been active proponents of the system, in some cases bringing the approach to management's attention directly and recommending that the company consider installing it.

The Duties of the Implementation Team

The Implementation Team's first responsibility is to understand the system as fully as possible. This is accomplished by providing them with a modified version of the training program that all managers will ultimately participate in. This session for the Implementation Team is modified to put more stress on the theory and philosophy and assumptions underlying the approach, and less on the mechanics and specific procedures to be followed, since their job will be to develop and tailor those procedures to their own organization's needs.

Their second responsibility is to concentrate on two primary areas: the development of policies and procedures, and the assurance of understanding and support. To carry out their role more effectively, the full Implementation Team is now subdivided into two task forces—the Policy Task Force and the Communications Task Force—each narrowing its focus to concentrate on one of the two areas.

The mission of the Policy Task Force is to develop a Discipline Without Punishment policy statement and procedural guidelines for initial approval by the Implementation Team as a whole and final approval by the organization's senior management. They are also charged with the responsibility to develop the procedures needed to measure, monitor, and maintain Discipline Without Punishment once it has been installed.

The other task force concentrates on communications. The members of this Communications Task Force function as a specialized advertising agency. Their product is their company's proprietary Discipline Without Punishment system that their counterparts on the Policy Task Force are creating. Their market is everyone in the organization who might be affected by the system. And their mission is to develop a communications plan that will ensure complete understanding, support, and acceptance by all.

There are several leadership positions to be filled. First, there is a need for a project manager. This role is most often filled by a senior human resources manager who has a full familiarity with the organization's current system and past practices. He or she serves as the primary liaison between the Implementation Team and the senior management group who will ultimately approve all of the Implementation Team's recommendations.

Next, there is an Implementation Team chairman. This position is usually filled by a senior line manager who brings not only a great deal of operating experience but also a depth of personal and organizational credibility. The Implementation Team chairman provides resources to the task force chairmen and is responsible for overall project scheduling and control.

Each task force must have a chairman assigned or appointed. While there are no specific criteria for selection, this is an ideal developmental opportunity for an individual in the organization who is seen as having a great deal of growth potential. Assuming a leadership role on an important special project is one of the most effective nonclassroom developmental activities available. Task force chairmen and members are responsible for most of the work done in the course of a Discipline Without Punishment implementation.

The Policy Task Force

The specific issues that will be addressed by the Policy Task Force are these:

- To whom does Discipline Without Punishment apply? (Can a vice president get a Written Reminder?)
- How many formal levels of discipline can an individual receive? Under what circumstances can an individual receive more than one Oral Reminder?
- How long should formal levels of discipline remain active? And should the time frame be longer as the level of seriousness increases?
- Should we provide for disciplinary incidents to be deactivated? And exactly what does *deactivation* mean?
- Who must approve at each level of the procedure? Who must be advised after a step has been taken?
- Will employees on an active step of disciplinary action be eligible for promotion? Can they get merit increases? Can they request a transfer to another department?
- How will crisis situations be handled?

- What will the specific documentation requirements be? Where will the documentation be kept? Who will get copies?
- What will happen to employees who are on an active step of disciplinary action under our old system at the time the new program goes into effect?

There will be more issues that will come up as they work on tailoring the generic Discipline Without Punishment system to the specific needs and culture and history of their company.

The Communications Task Force

The Communications Task Force faces a similarly demanding assignment:

- How should we position the decision to adopt Discipline Without Punishment? Is it a major new program with all the attendant bells and whistles? Part of our ongoing cultural change efforts? Or simply another example that this is a good place to work?
- What official communication has taken place so far? What rumors are afoot? What's the word on the grapevine about what we're doing?
- What should be the timing of future communications? How often do we need to communicate? What media are available?
- What resources are available for communication?
- What misunderstandings about Discipline Without Punishment are likely to arise? How can we discover them quickly? How can we correct them or put them to rest?
- What is the appropriate role of top management during the implementation process? Should they have any involvement with the training program? What will be their role once the system is in place?
- What needs to be included in the training to make it specifically appropriate for our company? What previous training efforts will the Discipline Without Punishment training program need to mesh with?
- What information will nonmanagement employees need

about the system? How will they get it? Who will give it to them?

The two task forces use these lists to begin their work of moving from the current system to the Discipline Without Punishment approach. In developing their recommendations, they follow a systematic five-step procedure:

1. Regarding this issue, what are all of the questions we need to answer?
2. What do we need to think about in answering each question? What are all of the issues involved? (Issues will include such considerations as past practice, the organization's future directions, just cause consideration, corporate culture, perceptions of managers and employees, ease of administration, and, perhaps most important, common sense).
3. What are the various alternatives available? (It is here that having access to the experience of other organizations is particularly useful.)
4. What are the pros and cons of each alternative?
5. Given all of the above, what is the balanced best recommendation we can make?

The Implementation Team's work usually takes between six and twelve weeks, depending on the availability of members to meet regularly and to complete individual assignments between meetings. In most cases, the individual Policy and Communications Task Forces will have two or three working sessions between each full meeting of the whole Implementation Team. Task force meetings usually last one to three hours as participants deal with specific issues and wrestle with the various approaches and recommendations. The meetings of the entire Implementation Team are usually scheduled for a full day.

While the number of meetings of the Implementation Team will vary from one organization to another, as a rule of thumb it is worthwhile to estimate that there will be five, each of which will consume a full day. The agenda for the first three of these meetings is predictable:

Implementation Team Meeting 1

- Training session on the philosophy and mechanics of Discipline Without Punishment
- Review of the role and responsibility of the Implementation Team
- Assignment of Implementation Team members to either the Policy or the Communications Task Force
- Appointment of task force chairmen
- Initial task force working session

The second meeting is held typically two to four weeks later.

Implementation Team Meeting 2

- A list of all questions that will need to be resolved (Policy Task Force)
- Initial/preliminary answers to each of the above questions. (Policy Task Force)
- Description of the overall communications plan (Communications Task Force)
- Recommendations on formal employee communication and format and content (Communications Task Force)
- List of issues for consideration by the entire Implementation Team (both task forces)

The third meeting takes place typically two to four weeks later.

Implementation Team Meeting 3

- Final recommendations on all remaining policy and procedural issues (Policy Task Force)
- Final draft of policy for review (Policy Task Force)
- Recommendations regarding transition procedures (Policy Task Force)
- Recommendations regarding forms (Policy Task Force)
- Proposed outline for employee communication session (Communications Task Force)
- Samples of any additional communications materials (Communications Task Force)
- Recommendations on any adjustments necessary to the Disci-

pline Without Punishment management training program (Communications Task Force)

The fourth meeting of the Implementation Team will come shortly before the beginning of the management training programs. Between the third and fourth meetings all of the recommendations from both task forces will be reviewed and approved (or returned with recommendations for revision) by the senior management group. The executive group will have confirmed communications plans and will have read and approved the final draft of the policy. The work of the project manager in keeping policy-level executives abreast of ongoing Implementation Team decisions and recommendations will help ensure that policy recommendations will be adopted as presented by the organization's senior management.

To increase organization-wide ownership and support, the policy statement and any procedural guidelines should clearly be marked as "draft materials" when they are presented to the company's supervisors and managers during the management training program. When organizations adopt new systems or procedures, a frequent and legitimate complaint is that the management group had no input.

By clearly indicating that these are in fact draft materials that will not be officially approved until all managers have had the chance to read and make recommendations for changes, the organization can significantly increase both the perception and the reality of ownership. The opportunity to recommend changes to the proposed Discipline Without Punishment policy is not mere window dressing. I can think of no organization in which the final policy and the accompanying procedural guidelines did not contain recommendations and suggestions made by supervisors during the management training program.

The fifth and final meeting of the Implementation Team comes immediately at the conclusion of the last management training seminar. The collection of suggested additions and deletions produced by seminar participants is circulated to all Implementation Team members. Each suggestion is reviewed and deliberated. The team makes its final decisions about any changes to the final draft policy that had earlier been approved by the executive group. They complete work on any other pieces of business that were either left over from the previous team meeting or arose during the management seminars, including the plans for monitoring and maintaining the system after implementation.

At this point, the work of the Implementation Team is almost complete. The only remaining major activity is conducting the employee communications sessions, the Communications Task Force's final duty.

When possible, it is appropriate for the Implementation Team members to meet with the senior management group both to make their recommendations on any final modifications to the draft policy and procedures and to be recognized by the organization's executive group for their success in arranging the transition to the new approach.

Management Training

The management training seminar to implement the Discipline Without Punishment program usually consumes two full days. In addition to gaining the skills necessary to handle one of the most difficult parts of their jobs effectively, managers must also understand and accept the new philosophy that underlies the procedures they are learning and skills they are acquiring. Even with a skilled trainer and an enthusiastic audience, the task of transferring all of the knowledge, attitudes, and skills is daunting.

The objectives for the training sessions are straightforward. By the end of the workshop, each participant needs to be able to do the following:

- Conduct effective "Positive Contact" discussions with subordinates and use other recognition techniques to improve employee morale and encourage good performance.
- Identify and describe the difference between actual performance and expected performance in a specific and objective way.
- Distinguish between problems caused by deficiencies in knowledge and deficiencies in execution, and use the most appropriate strategies for resolving each.
- For any performance problem, identify the good business rea-

sons why it must be solved and the logical consequences the employee will face if it is not corrected.

- Conduct effective discussions with employees that result in the individual's agreement to change.
- Document all transactions properly, both informal Coaching Sessions and formal levels of the Discipline Without Punishment procedure.
- Conduct formal disciplinary transactions at each level of the Discipline Without Punishment procedure (Oral Reminder, Written Reminder, Decision Making Leave) properly and confidently.
- Understand the specific mechanics of the organization's Discipline Without Punishment system sufficiently well so as to be able to make recommendations to the Implementation Team on ways in which the policy or procedures could be made more effective.
- Answer common questions from employees about the operation and philosophy of the system and explain why the company decided to invest in this program.
- Understand, accept, and enthusiastically support the nonpunitive Discipline Without Punishment philosophy in all performance management activity.

The actual content of the seminar will vary greatly, based on the needs of the organization and their previous management development efforts. The greatest chunk of seminar time, however, needs to be spent having managers actually practice holding effective discussions with subordinates. Other major topics to which most organizations choose to devote a great deal of time include recognition of good performance, the review of the final drafts of the policy and procedural guidelines (including the solicitation of recommendations to the Implementation Team), and a discussion of the requirements needed to make the transition to the new system successful.

"But Where's the Pound of Flesh?"

Besides giving managers the skills to handle people problems effectively, a constant if subtle objective of the management seminar is the development of acceptance of the nonpunitive philosophy on the part of all participants. Old ways die hard. Both in convincing senior managers to adopt the Discipline Without Punishment system, and in convincing managers to give up their old ways and deal with troublemakers with dignity and grace, a lot of emotional resistance must often be overcome.

A major American city was considering implementing Discipline Without Punishment for all city employees. Around the conference table sat the senior management group: the city manager and a deputy; the city attorney; the head of human resources; and two or three other senior operating officials.

As I explained the operation of the system, the reasons other cities had implemented it and the results they had achieved, the city attorney showed more and more signs of distress. His head nodded as I answered all of his questions and explained all of the reasons why Discipline Without Punishment would be more effective than the traditional approach they were currently using.

But while it was obvious that he fully understood and appreciated the logical and rational reasons why Discipline Without Punishment was a better way of dealing with people than the approach that they had used for years, his heart wasn't in it. The logic was clear, but an emotional barrier was preventing his accepting the approach.

He asked one question after another: What about this, how would you handle that? Would you ever suspend a person without pay for a week or two if the steps of the Discipline Without Punishment approach failed to convince him to change? No, I responded, once a person has been through all the steps of Discipline Without Punishment and continues to perform unacceptably, termination's the appropriate response. Isn't it true that some people change as a result of punishment? Yes, that's true, I replied. But implementing Discipline Without Punishment reflects an organization's decision to eliminate punishment as a way of managing people, even though some people may respond better to being punished than to being forced to take personal responsibility for their own behavior.

Finally, even though all of his questions had been answered and the logic of the system was apparent, he was still unconvinced. He shook his head, then looked directly at me and blurted out, "But where's the pound of flesh?"

At that moment I realized that he had identified the biggest obstacle that managers must overcome in embracing a nonpunitive approach to handling disciplinary action. Even though I had been working with organizations and their managers for twenty years to help them both understand the approach and install it effectively, in that moment I finally understood the most basic reservation that some managers have about Discipline Without Punishment: There is no pound of flesh.

No benefit comes without its price. I had always considered Discipline Without Punishment to be an approach that was cost-free, except for the direct dollars and time invested by the organization to install the approach. But the city attorney had identified a very real cost that I had never considered: the cost of giving up the ability to settle the score with someone who had misbehaved.

The city attorney had put his finger on a rarely admitted but deeply felt need of many managers: to respond in kind to inappropriate organizational behavior. When an employee misbehaves, comes to work late, confronts citizens or customers with a hostile attitude and a chip on the shoulder, a manager often wants more than simply a correction of the problem and a commitment to future good performance. *Often he wants revenge.*

This atavistic need to settle the score is the price managers pay for implementing Discipline Without Punishment. They get improved performance, a deeper commitment to the organization and its expectations, but they don't get revenge. Granted, there are times when the desire for revenge is very strong in all of us. It can take every ounce of maturity we've got to turn loose from our need for that pound of flesh and be satisfied merely with solved problems and enhanced relationships.

Building Management Commitment

The implementation seminar usually closes by having participants anticipate their transition back to the workplace and the way in which they will explain the Discipline Without Punishment system when they are asked about it (as most of them will be). Working in teams they identify the most difficult, most embarrassing, most disconcerting questions they feel they might be asked by their employees when they return to their workplaces. Some of the questions they generate deal with the procedural mechanics of the Discipline Without Punishment system (how many Written Reminders can I get, what if I get sick on my Decision Making Leave day?). Most, however, concern far more substantive issues. The great majority of the questions they raise usually reveal issues that they may not yet have fully resolved for themselves:

- At a time when the company is talking about the need to cut costs, why are we investing so much money in a program like this?
- Isn't this just a quicker way to get rid of people?
- I never create any disciplinary problems. What's in this for me?
- I've seen lots of programs come and go. Isn't this going to be just another good idea that gets off to a big start and then fades away and is forgotten?
- Why do we need to have a discipline system anyway?
- These new steps are just the same old thing with new names. There's nothing really new here, is there?
- I like what you say about recognizing those people who do a good job, but do you really think that's going to happen?
- What will happen to a manager who doesn't follow this program, who keeps on acting like he's always acted? And what about the manager who sees people doing their jobs wrong and goofing off and doesn't say anything about it. . . . Will anything happen to him?

Each team then answers the questions thrown at them from the others. When participants discover that they are able to answer whatever question they are asked convincingly and forthrightly, they also discover that they have incorporated the essence of Discipline Without Punishment. They may not know all of the mechanics, and they will soon forget many of the specific details. But their subordinates are not usually concerned with testing the boss to see if he can remember everything that he was taught in charm school. What subordinates really want to know from those to whom they look for leadership is: What do you think about this? Are you really committed to it? Do you believe that this will really make a difference and make this a better place for me to work?

Once the manager discovers that he is fully capable of answering that question, not from his head but from his heart, it is time to close the proceedings and send the participants on their way. The seminar has done its job.

Moving Toward Implementation

Once all of the organization's supervisors and managers have completed the management seminar, the Implementation Team meets for its final session. The agenda for this session is to resolve all of the questions and issues that were raised by the participants in the management seminars.

The issues brought up to the Implementation Team range from the most mundane—a typographical error, an obvious miswording—to substantive matters that require genuine discussion and provoke difficult decisions. If there have been several management training seminars, as there invariably are in large organizations, it is important that Implementation Team members be present in every one. When Implementation Team members are sprinkled throughout the seminars, they can share with their colleagues the rationale the team used in arriving at the many procedural decisions they made. Equally important, they can bring back to the team a full explanation of any of their colleagues' concerns or recommendations.

The ideal close for the final Implementation Team meeting is a presentation by team members to the organization's senior staff concerning the final policy recommendations and implementation plans. The official date for the start of the new program will be confirmed and the plans for monitoring and measuring the results will be reviewed. Finally, team members will be recognized for their efforts in creating the system.

Three more major activities must still take place before the official implementation date of the system: the executive orientation session, the employee orientation program, and the individual notification to people who are on an active step of disciplinary action under the old system of their status once the new system goes into effect.

Executive Orientation

One concern invariably raised by participants in the management seminars is whether top management will actually support the efforts of lower-level managers who use the system well and make the tough calls required for any discipline procedure to work right. While they may not have personally experienced the situation, they have all heard horror stories of managers who, despite accumulating a great store of documentation of an individual's continuing failure to meet organizational standards, were rebuked and reversed in their attempt to gain approval to terminate. Even though the factual content of many of these stories varies widely when closely checked out, managers still perceive upper management as being unsympathetic to the day-to-day employee problems they have to deal with.

It would be nice if the entire senior management group would participate in each management seminar as regular enrollees and not as short-time, drop-in observers (and the depth of commitment in many organizations is such that all senior managers do take part in the full two-day program). However, the needs of top executives are sufficiently different from the needs of middle managers and supervisors, for whom the management seminar is designed, that their inability to be regular participants is not a significant obstacle to program success. Senior managers almost never conduct disciplinary discussions.

What senior managers do need to do is coach middle managers and supervisors on their expectations of high organizational performance and their insistence that all of the techniques and procedures and skills acquired in the seminar be used as presented.

Instead of their attending the two-day management seminar, a more effective and convenient approach for top management is to schedule a three-hour executive orientation program, typically conducted by a combination of the facilitator for the training programs, the Discipline Without Punishment project manager, and the chairman of the Implementation Team. The objectives of this session, tailored to meet the specific needs of the members of the executive group, include enabling them to:

- Understand completely all of the policy and procedural elements of the organization's proprietary Discipline Without Punishment program as tailored and modified by the Implementation Team.

- Understand the importance of and accept the responsibility for:
  - Using the appropriate terminology (e.g., never referring to an Oral Reminder as a "verbal reprimand")
  - Using all elements of the system in his own personal performance management actions
  - Holding subordinate managers accountable for using and administering the system correctly
- Coach their subordinate managers in the proper use of the system.
- Recognize when subordinate managers are using the Discipline Without Punishment system properly, and recognize and reinforce their activities appropriately.
- Recognize when subordinate managers are not using the Discipline Without Punishment system properly, and provide the necessary coaching and other corrective action to change their use of the program.
- Understand, accept, and enthusiastically support the nonpunitive nature of the organization's "Discipline Without Punishment" philosophy.

Employee Orientation Program

For most of an organization's employees, the only contact they will directly have with the Discipline Without Punishment system is when their conscientious performance is recognized in a Positive Contact or similar transaction. They will be affected indirectly by the system when they discover that their poorer-performing colleagues are confronted with the demand for change, and that the few who do not accept that responsibility disappear.

They will be able to tell that the system is working when they sense that morale around the place is higher. They will know that things are different when their supervisors give them specific directions and more useful feedback, instead of merely saying "Do your best" or "Try harder."

But they will probably not be aware of the intimate mechanics of the Discipline Without Punishment procedure since they will never experience any of the formal steps of the discipline system. However, it is important that all members of the organization be familiarized with the entire procedure since one of the great benefits of the approach is the peace of mind that it provides to all organization members. They know that in case they ever do become embroiled in a disciplinary scrape, they will be dealt with with dignity, will have the chance to emerge from it with their pride intact, and ultimately will have their record cleansed.

For this reason, most organizations schedule an orientation program to introduce all employees to the overall Discipline Without Punishment procedure. By this time there have been several announcements and updates produced by the Communications Task Force over the course of the implementation process. This session, which generally need take only one hour, is the major communications vehicle to ensure organization-wide understanding of the approach and the reasons for adopting it.

Some organizations choose to make the implementation of the Discipline Without Punishment system a major event. They may produce a videotape that explains the company's rationale for moving away from an adversarial approach and into a system that focuses on decision making and personal responsibility. The steps of the system are usually reviewed in detail, and the company's commitment to recognizing good performance is emphasized. Some companies use outside narrators and actors and engage professional producers (or make use of their own equivalent internal resources) to produce a broadcast-quality tape.

Lower-budget, simpler video approaches can be just as effective. A large chemical company, in spite of abundant resources, put a single camera on a tripod and pointed it at the senior operating manager, a man of tremendous integrity and credibility. He stood next to a flimsy flip chart on which he had personally written the core concepts of Discipline Without Punishment. The camera recorded him as he talked simply and directly, telling every member of the organization why he had decided to adopt this system and why he believed in it. He expressed his bone-deep conviction that once every person out there got familiar with it they would believe in it just as strongly as he did. It was a performance that no amount of Hollywood slick could make any more credible.

Whether highlighted by a superb video production or just a simple meeting led by the members of the Implementation Team, the objectives of the employee orientation program are the same. By the end of this session, each employee should:

- Understand the reasons that the organization chose to implement a program that emphasizes decision making and personal responsibility.
- Understand the mechanics of each element of the company's Discipline Without Punishment system (Positive Contact, Coaching Session, Oral Reminder, Written Reminder, Decision Making Leave).
- Understand the specific benefits to him in the new system (the "What's in it for me?" question).
- Understand how Discipline Without Punishment integrates with other organizational efforts to improve the culture and quality of work life.
- Understand, accept, and enthusiastically support the nonpunitive—that is, "Discipline Without Punishment"—philosophy of the program.

Individual Meetings

Shortly before the system's official implementation date, individual meetings are held with each person who has received a formal disciplinary transaction during the last year or so. Each of these individuals is advised what decision has been made about where he stands under the new system.

Deciding on transition procedures is another important responsibility for the Implementation Team. From the moment that the organization decides to install Discipline Without Punishment and commences the implementation process, detailed records should be kept of every disciplinary transaction that occurs. In addition, a search of the records should be made to identify all members of the organization who have received disciplinary action in the recent past so that all cases can be considered in moving to the new approach. While the organization may not have had a formal "active period" under the previous system, every person who has received a formal disciplinary transaction in the past year or two will remember that fact and will be concerned about what his status will be once the new system goes into place.

There are three alternatives available to the Implementation Team in deciding what to do about individuals who are on active disciplinary steps at the time of transition to the new system. First, they can wipe the slate clean for everyone (everyone gets a fresh start). Second, they can reduce each discipline step one level (an active written warning under the old system becomes an active Oral Reminder once the new system is installed). Finally, they can maintain everyone under the new system at the same place they were under the old (a person with an active written warning under the old system now has an active Written Reminder).

Implementation Teams usually begin the decision-making process by determining how many people are on active steps of disciplinary action, who these people are, and at what level in the system they are. If there is a reasonably small number of individuals and they are not clustered at the final level of disciplinary action, then it would be a major gesture of good faith on the organization's part to wipe the slate clean for everybody. The experience of most organizations that have elected to wipe slates clean universally is that there is little correlation between the people who get their slates wiped clean and those who get into disciplinary scrapes following the new system's inauguration.

If there is a larger number of individuals on active disciplinary steps, if these individuals are clustered at the more serious end of the disciplinary action scale, and if there are a couple of genuine miscreants for whom it would be a serious error to allow them to return to zero, the approach of "everybody take one step back" makes sense.

In this situation there would be no one who enters the system at the Decision Making Leave level, even if an individual had previously received more than one suspension. Anyone who was previously at a final-step level would now be at the Written Reminder stage and eligible for a Decision Making Leave if a disciplinary problem arose again. Those who had previously received a written warning would now be considered to be at the Oral Reminder stage.

While it might be possible, it would certainly be difficult to justify moving individuals in lockstep from the former system to an equivalent level of the new Discipline Without Punishment procedure. It is doubtful, too, whether any arbitrator or other third party could be convinced of the appropriateness of that decision. Even organizations that insist absolutely on personal responsibility and decision making find a place for mercy. This is the place.

Once the decision about how the transition will be handled has been made by the Implementation Team and approved by senior management, it becomes the responsibility of individual supervisors to advise each of their subordinates who are on active discipline steps what their status will be at the time of the new system's inauguration. The Implementation Team, assisted by the human resources function, usually prepares a script for the supervisor to follow, telling the employee what his current status is and communicating the supervisor's expectation that the employee will never again commit any disciplinary offense. This message is particularly important when the company has generously decided to let bygones be bygones and provide a fresh start for all.

Choosing an Implementation Date

Frankly, the date itself makes little difference.

No matter how long the Implementation Team spends in developing the policies and procedures, the timing of the overall project is not particularly critical until the management training programs begin. It is desirable to have all management seminars scheduled as close together as possible. Several organizations have used teams of trainers and scheduled management training sessions concurrently so that all the training could be done in the shortest possible period.

Once the final management training program has been completed, the amount of energy in the organization for moving into the new system will be at a peak. It would be a mistake to allow this to dissipate by unduly delaying the actual starting date of the program. In the seminars, managers ask about when they can start using the procedures and complain when told that while they can begin holding Coaching Sessions immediately, no formal disciplinary transactions using the Discipline Without Punishment steps should begin until the official implementation date. (Managers then either go ahead and take the steps anyway, or delay taking appropriate action until the new system goes into effect. If the time between the final training session and the official inauguration of the system is elongated, a rush of disciplinary conversations may transpire in the first weeks of the new system's start.)

In a recent implementation at a large Columbia/HCA Healthcare hospital, however, the Implementation Team decided to encourage managers to use all elements of the system immediately after training, without waiting for the official implementation date that had been set. Instead of viewing the implementation date as the day on which all managers could begin using the new procedures, the Implementation Team decided that this was the day after which they were no longer allowed to use any of the elements of their previous system. This approach made sense and will probably continue to be a recommendation in future implementations of Discipline Without Punishment.

From the last management seminar until the first day of the new system, the following events must occur:

- All recommendations and suggestions from the participants in the management seminars must be collected, organized, and circulated for review to all members of the Implementation Team.
- The Implementation Team must hold its final meeting and resolve each issue coming out of the management seminars, including transition plans and the development of a system to measure and maintain the Discipline Without Punishment program once it goes into effect.
- The recommendations of the Implementation Team, plus the final drafts of all policy statements and procedural elements of the system must be approved by senior management.
- The executive orientation program must be scheduled and conducted.
- The employee orientation programs must be scheduled and conducted.
- All administrative materials and forms must be printed and circulated.
- Each employee on an active step of discipline under the previous system must be advised of his status under the new system.

It is certainly feasible to accomplish all of the above activities in three or four weeks' time, particularly if the organization moves rapidly, accomplishes various tasks concurrently, and lays the groundwork for these activities well before the management seminars begin.

Measuring the Effectiveness of Discipline Without Punishment

As soon as implementation day arrives, the program for monitoring and maintaining the system goes into effect. During the previous months of work by the Implementation Team, they should have been collecting as much data as possible on the activities and effectiveness of the old system for use as a basis of comparison with the new.

There are three aspects that an effective measurement plan considers: (1) the nature and amount of activity that occurs under the new system, (2) the reactions and perceptions of organizational members, and (3) the operating and human resources results that can be attributed to the system.

The determination of what to measure should be made in conjunction with the senior management team, taking into account the ease with which data can be collected and the resources available to devote to the measurement effort. What will senior management accept as evidence that the system is working effectively? A reduction in the number of disciplinary incidents may not be a true measure of success if the organization was previously managed so loosely that anything less than a physical assault was met with little more than a dark glance and the admonition to knock it off.

For most organizations, however, a reduction in disciplinary action is a mark of success. A better indicator could be a reduction in the number of people who proceed from one disciplinary level to a more serious level. Almost always, a reduction in discharges is beneficial (although the reverse may be true for organizations that previously provided ensurance of lifetime tenure regardless of performance or behavior).

Tracking all of the data on the amount and type of disciplinary activity, particularly the number of Positive Contacts and coaching sessions, will not only provide an indicator of system use but also highlight those sections or departments that are experiencing significantly more or less activity than other organizational units. Whether this is good or bad will require direct investigation, but locating potential problem areas will be greatly facilitated.

It may be particularly important to measure the number of official Positive Contact transactions. One of the primary reasons organizations decide to implement the Discipline Without Punishment system is to move toward an environment where good performance is frequently recognized and reinforced. After an initial flurry, supervisors often fail to maintain their good intentions of regularly recognizing good performance. But if they are required to report the number of transactions they have had on a quarterly basis, for example, there is an added incentive to continue what they know they should be doing anyway.

Besides simply counting the number of incidents of each element in the system, another important area to measure is the reaction of organization members to the system. How do they feel about it? Would they go back to the old way?

Either as part of the initial implementation process, or as an early activity in the management seminars, many organizations conduct a survey to determine the reaction of organization members to the company's current performance management activities. If designed properly, this same survey can be readministered six months or a year after installation to see if the perceptions of people have changed. Questions covering these areas are reasonably easy to construct and respond to using a 1–5 or similar scale:

Are people whose performance is unacceptable confronted with the need to change?

Are people whose performance is above average recognized for their contributions?

Do managers feel confident in their ability to hold productive disciplinary or coaching discussions?

When a supervisor recommends termination, does senior management usually support the recommendation?

Is the amount of paperwork required by the system excessive?

Is the relationship between nonmanagement employees and company managers pleasant, professional, and respectful?

In addition to specifically constructed surveys, any existing employee attitude data can provide valuable information about the perceptions of organization members in the area of how their performance is measured.

Managing and Maintaining Discipline Without Punishment

"We're up to 35,000 feet at 625 knots," the copilot told the captain of the 747. "We can turn the engines off now."

Of course, you can't turn the engines off—not for a Discipline Without Punishment program any more than for a 747. And not even after Discipline Without Punishment is fully launched and flying high. Systems don't fail because they weren't well designed or well implemented. Systems fail for two reasons: no ownership and poor maintenance.

The ownership issue has been dealt with by using an Implementation Team to create the policies and procedures, and by not making the policy official until all managers were given the chance to propose revisions. Making sure that the system is continually well maintained helps guarantee that initial success will continue.

From the first day of implementation the system will begin to deteriorate. Supervisors who were experts on holding effective coaching conversations and disciplinary transactions at the end of the seminar find that their skills rapidly atrophy if they are not frequently used. Managers who could answer any question about policy administration the day after the seminar are hard pressed to respond when a month has gone by. New supervisors join the organization to replace departees; Implementation Team members move on. As attention to the system necessarily becomes reduced in the weeks and months and years following the rush of energy that accompanies implementation, plans must be drafted and carried out to ensure that skills and awareness are maintained at high levels. The employee handbook must be revised to incorporate information about the approach. The employee orientation program needs a section to let new employees know that, should performance problems ever develop, they can expect to be treated differently here than they would be in a less desirable place to work.

As the supervisory population changes, plans for a repetition of the original training program for new supervisors and refresher training for existing supervisors must be made and carried out. The videotapes, posters, and booklets that may have been prepared to explain the program at the beginning should not gather dust in the closet forever.

At some point, however, an organization's reduction in high-profile attention to Discipline Without Punishment ceases to be a matter for concern. This occurs when the system is imperceptibly transformed from a mere "program" to a fully integrated aspect of life in the organization.

As part of my research for this book and almost two decades after I had developed the Discipline Without Punishment approach at Frito-Lay, I returned to the company to find out whether the system I had created was still in place. While I had maintained close relationships with many Frito-Lay colleagues in the years since I had left the company to begin my consulting practice, I had never been back in any professional capacity.

In some twenty years as a consultant helping organizations develop their own nonpunitive systems based on the work I did at Frito-Lay, I had always been able to say with confidence, "No company that I have ever worked with to implement Discipline Without Punishment has ever abandoned it." I wanted to be able to continue to say that.

I was nervous when I drove into Frito-Lay corporate headquarters to talk with Terry Taillard, the corporate director of training and development, the same job I had when Discipline Without Punishment was born. I had good reason to be nervous. When I had phoned Taillard earlier to ask about Frito-Lay's current use of Discipline Without Punishment, he said that he wasn't familiar with a program by that name.

I met Taillard in the cafeteria. As we sat by a window overlooking the handsome grounds of what many consider to be the most beautiful corporate campus in the United States, my anxiety disappeared when he explained his perplexing earlier statement about Discipline Without Punishment. "Oh, we use it everywhere in the company. I just didn't know it had a name. It's just the way we do business here."

The final test of the effectiveness and success of Discipline Without Punishment is when it stops being a program . . . a project

. . . a policy. Discipline Without Punishment is finally and fully implemented when it has become so incorporated into the grain of organizational life that everyone considers it, "just the way we do business here."

Index

About the Author

Dick Grote is president of Grote Consulting in Dallas, Texas, where he is also adjunct professor of management at the University of Dallas Graduate School of Management. His firm helps companies implement Discipline Without Punishment and other performance management systems.